READER'S DIGEST BASIC GUIDE

Working with Bricks, Concrete and Stone

Contents

Bricks and bricklaying 2
BUYING, ESTIMATING, MORTAR, TOOLS, CUTTING BRICKS, TYPES OF BOND,
CAVITY WALLS, DAMP-PROOF COURSES, FOUNDATIONS, DECORATIVE WORK, RENDERING

Projects 19
PAVING AND PATHS, WALLS, PERGOLAS AND SCREENS, GARDEN POOLS, BARBECUE

Concrete and cement 27
INGREDIENTS, TOOLS, ESTIMATING, DIFFERENT MIXES, READY-MIXED CONCRETE,
MIXING BY HAND, USING A MIXER, PREPARING THE SITE, CASTING SLABS, LAYING FLOORS,
PRE-CAST CONCRETE, BLOCK AND SCREEN WALLS

Stone and stonework 40
BUYING, PREPARING AND CLEANING, LAYING PATHS, FOUNDATIONS, FIREPLACE KITS

Repairs 43
REPOINTING, DAMAGED BRICKWORK, DECAYED STONEWORK, EFFLORESCENCE,
SETTLEMENT, CHIMNEY STACKS, CONDENSATION, CONCRETE PATHS AND STEPS

THE TEXT AND ILLUSTRATIONS IN THIS BOOK ARE TAKEN
FROM 'THE READER'S DIGEST COMPLETE DO-IT-YOURSELF MANUAL'
PUBLISHED BY THE READER'S DIGEST ASSOCIATION LIMITED
LONDON   NEW YORK   CAPE TOWN   MONTREAL   SYDNEY

Bricks and bricklaying/1

The right bricks for the job

Kentish stocks, Staffordshire blues, gaults, wirecuts, commons and Flettons are just a few of the several hundred names used to describe different types of bricks. For practical purposes, however, it is enough to know the basic distinction between facings, commons and engineering bricks.

Facings are used for brickwork that will be visible in the finished structure, most typically the external faces of houses. Pleasant appearance and good weathering properties are the basic requirements of facings. They can be rough or smooth-textured, hard or soft, and in shades that vary from light red, through the yellows and browns, to purple or black.

Facing bricks can be deceptively tough, and have good weather-resisting qualities. Many of them are virtually indestructible, even though they are soft and porous.

Commons, which are cheaper, are used for 'non-visible' brickwork, such as walls that will be plastered or rendered over. Some commons, however, are attractive and can be used as facings.

Engineering bricks are hard and impervious to water, and are usually reserved for underground structures such as manholes or where unusual conditions call for something extra tough and waterproof.

Bricks of all these three types are graded by quality—internal, ordinary and special. Facings are either special or ordinary; commons are almost always internal quality; and engineering bricks are usually special quality.

Other terms used to describe types of bricks indicate how they are made, what they are made from, and where they are manufactured.

'Stocks', for example, are clay bricks made in various districts: Kentish stocks are usually yellow, while Dorking stocks are made in various shades of pink, or are multi-coloured. They may be either commons or facings.

Flettons are named from the Huntingdonshire village where they originated and can be either plain-faced commons or textured and coloured facings.

In view of the confusion of brick names, the best and easiest way to ensure that you buy the right bricks for your needs is to ask the advice of your supplier—either the manufacturer or the builders' merchant.

If you want to match a new extension or a garage with an existing house, ask the supplier to have a look at the job on the site. Even if the brickwork of the house is old and weathered, he should be able to suggest new bricks that will tone in. For example, grey bricks can match weathered yellow stocks of Victorian houses. Demolition yards often hold stocks of interesting-looking second-hand bricks which may suit a specific job.

How many do you need ?

Almost all bricks now conform to the British Standards size of 215 mm. long, 65 mm. high and 102·5 mm. wide.

Counting in the mortar joints between bricks, this gives a 'working' or 'nominal' size of $225 \times 112 \cdot 5 \times 75$ mm. Always use this nominal size when working out the size of structures. For instance, if you are planning to build a wall 3375 mm. long, divide this by the 225 mm. nominal brick length, the answer being 15. Each course or layer of bricks will thus consist of 15 bricks laid end to end, and each course will raise the height of the wall by 75 mm.

Try to keep the length of brick structures to multiples of 225 or 112·5 mm. Working to these brick and half-brick sizes saves a lot of unnecessary brick cutting and makes for a neater appearance.

Similarly, keep all heights to multiples of 75 mm. Each square metre, or metre super, of 112·5 mm. thick brickwork requires 60 bricks, but it is usual to add 10% to the estimated number required for cutting and wastage.

If you are planning to use non-standard bricks, order them well in advance: they are made up only in economic batches.

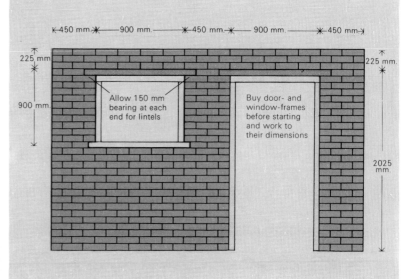

Planning a brick structure. Try to make all measurements multiples of brick dimensions. Subtract from the total number of bricks required the space to be occupied by windows and doors; and a dozen or so bricks for breakages.

Labels in figure: 450 mm. — 900 mm. — 450 mm. — 900 mm. — 450 mm.; 225 mm; 900 mm.; Allow 150 mm bearing at each end for lintels; Buy door- and window-frames before starting and work to their dimensions; 225 mm.; 2025 mm.

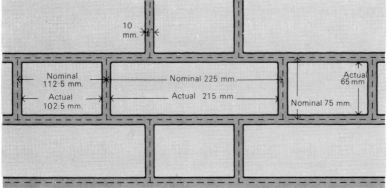

Ordering and estimating. Ignore the actual size of bricks and work from the nominal sizes. The difference is accounted for by 10 mm. (⅜ in.) mortar jointing.

Labels in figure: 10 mm. ⅜"; Nominal 112·5 mm.; Actual 102·5 mm.; Nominal 225 mm.; Actual 215 mm.; Actual 65 mm; Nominal 75 mm.

Stack bricks safely by allowing the end 'walls' to slope inward towards the top.

Label in figure: Stack the bulk of the bricks on edge

Useful shapes for neat finishing

Bricks of a shape other than the basic 225 × 112·5 × 75 mm. block are known as specials. Some of the more useful types for do-it-yourself work are: bullnoses, used for steps and edgings; coping bricks for the top courses of boundary walls; and curved bricks for arches, curved walls and ornamental wells. There are even minia- tures (down to 22 mm. thick) for fireplaces, niches and other decorative features inside and outside the house.

It is also useful to be able to recognise specials you may want to replace when repairing brickwork.

Bats and closers, which are technically specials, are cut as required. Others must be ordered well in advance, as there may be delays in delivery—in fact, if you plan to build in the summer, January may be a good time to place your order.

Do not confuse the term 'special' with 'special facings'. Special facings are facing bricks with particular load-bearing and weather-resistant properties.

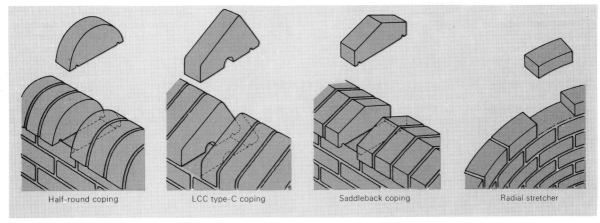

Half-round coping   LCC type-C coping   Saddleback coping   Radial stretcher

Copings are weatherproof as well as giving an attractive appearance to walls. Curved bricks can be used to make attractive pathways.

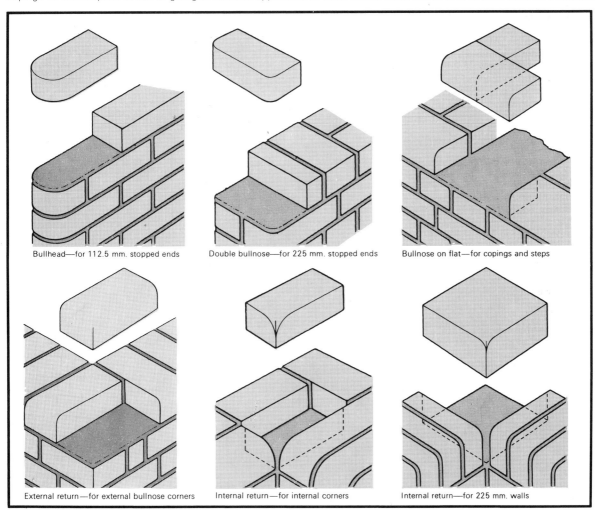

Bullhead—for 112.5 mm. stopped ends   Double bullnose—for 225 mm. stopped ends   Bullnose on flat—for copings and steps

External return—for external bullnose corners   Internal return—for internal corners   Internal return—for 225 mm. walls

Step-edgings, neat finishes to the tops and ends of walls, plinths and borders, can all be devised by imaginative use of 'specials'.

Bricks and bricklaying/3

Types of mortar

Mortars are composed of a binder—cement, lime or a mixture of the two—and a fine aggregate, usually sand. The proportions are usually one part binder to three parts sand, but various mixes within these limits are used, according to the material to be bonded, the weather during building, the strength needed by the finished structure and the exposure it will undergo.

Mortar should be neither much stronger nor much weaker than the bricks or blocks it is used with.

Cement mortar sets quickly and is very strong, but settling movements and shrinkage in drying can cause it to crack.
Lime mortar is weak and hardens slowly, but takes up settling movements without cracking, and shrinkage cracks are finer than in cement mortar. Lime prevents bricks drawing water from mortar too fast for proper setting and adhesion.
Cement-lime mortar has largely replaced lime mortar as it is stronger and sets more quickly. The cement gives strength, while the lime reduces drying shrinkage and makes a workable mortar that is able to retain water.

Aerated mortar is cement mortar with an air-entraining plasticiser, such as Febmix, added. The plasticiser makes the mix more workable and allows the mortar to take up settling movements and to resist frost. It forms air bubbles that provide spaces for the water to expand into when it freezes, thus preventing cracking. Follow the instructions on the plasticiser tin.

Choosing the right mortar

The table below shows how equivalent mixes in various types of mortar can be used in various bricklaying jobs.

Cement mortar gives the strongest bond and resistance to rain penetration, but aerated mortar has the greatest resistance to freezing. Thus it can be seen from the table that a good general-purpose mortar for most weather conditions is a 1:1:6 cement-lime mix—1 part of Portland cement, 1 part of lime and 6 parts of clean sand. Measure all parts by volume.

When there is danger of frost during building or before the mortar is cured, use mortars listed for severely exposed walls.

Good quality hand-made bricks can be laid with 1:4 cement mortar, but check with the brick-maker in any case of doubt.

Equivalent mortar mixes

Type of brickwork	Cement mortar	Cement-lime mortar	Masonry cement mortar	Aerated mortar
Engineering bricks, retaining walls	1 part cement 3 parts sand			
Sills and copings	1 part cement 3 parts sand	1 part cement $\frac{1}{2}$ part lime $4\frac{1}{2}$ parts sand		
Free-standing walls, work below DPC, unrendered parapets	1 part cement 3 parts sand	1 part cement 1 part lime 6 parts sand	1 part masonry cement $4\frac{1}{2}$ parts sand	1 part cement 6 parts sand with plasticiser
Severely exposed walls above DPC, rendered parapets, inner leaf of cavity wall		1 part cement 1 part lime 6 parts sand	1 part masonry cement $4\frac{1}{2}$ parts sand	1 part cement 6 parts sand with plasticiser
Internal walls		1 part cement 2 parts lime 9 parts sand	1 part masonry cement 6 parts sand	1 part cement 8 parts sand with plasticiser

Using lime in mortar

The main types of lime are hydraulic, non-hydraulic and semi-hydraulic. Most limes are non-hydraulic or semi-hydraulic.

Hydraulic lime sets by combining with water and can set under water. Non-hydraulic lime hardens by drying out and then combining with atmospheric carbon dioxide.

Semi-hydraulic lime hardens chiefly by drying, but has some hydraulic properties.

All these types are sold as both hydrated lime and quicklime. Hydrated lime is much more convenient, as quicklime needs to be slaked.

Hydrated hydraulic lime must be used straight from the bag, but semi-hydraulic and non-hydraulic limes are made more workable by soaking them in water for at least 24 hours before use.

Soak hydrated lime by making it into lime putty or into a wet mixture with sand that is called 'coarse stuff'. Ready-mixed coarse stuff can be bought.

Make lime putty by adding lime to water in a clean container and stirring it to a thick, creamy consistency. Excess water separates to the top and can be drained off. Lime putty keeps for weeks while damp.

To make coarse stuff, mix the volumes of hydrated lime—or lime putty—and sand required for the mortar and add water to make a suitable consistency. Coarse stuff keeps for weeks if made into a smooth heap and kept covered with wet sacking. It can be used immediately if lime putty is used.

Mixing mortar

Mix cement mortar like concrete (see p. 31), making a plastic mixture that is damp enough to retain the impression of the trowel without crumbling, but is not runny. In a concrete mixer, a mix appears to be drier than it really is.

Make a note of the amount of water used in the first mix so that you can add the correct amount to later mixes.

Use clean, well-graded building sand. This contains grains of varying sizes in equal proportions by weight. Avoid sands whose grains are uniformly coarse or fine.

To mix cement-lime mortar, add cement to the coarse stuff, which stiffens while stored and must be knocked up thoroughly before use, though it should not need extra water.

A volume of coarse stuff is the same as the volume of sand it contains, because the lime fills the spaces between the grains of sand without adding to the volume.

Thus, when mixing a 1:1:6 cement-lime mortar, add 1 part of cement for every 6 parts of coarse stuff made from 1 part of lime and 6 parts of sand. Do not use 1 part of cement to 7 parts of coarse stuff.

Mortar must be used within two hours of being mixed.

Ready-mixed mortar: this needs only the addition of water and can save money when only a small amount is needed.

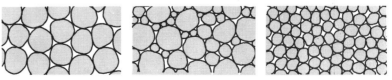

Use well-graded sand (centre). Grains should not be uniformly large (left) or small (right).

Basic bricklaying kit

The essential tools for straightforward bricklaying are few. Do not 'make do' by buying ill-considered 'bargains' or cheap offers; good tools are vital, especially a good-quality trowel.

This is what you need:

Brick trowel
Bolster
Club hammer
Long spirit level
Line and pins
Steel measuring tape or rule
Spot-boards (home-made)
Gauge-rod (home-made)
Builder's square (home-made)

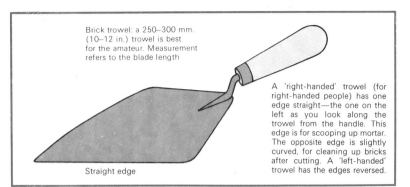

Brick trowel: a 250–300 mm. (10–12 in.) trowel is best for the amateur. Measurement refers to the blade length

A 'right-handed' trowel (for right-handed people) has one edge straight—the one on the left as you look along the trowel from the handle. This edge is for scooping up mortar. The opposite edge is slightly curved, for cleaning up bricks after cutting. A 'left-handed' trowel has the edges reversed.

Straight edge

Using a trowel

Handling a trowel properly is the key to quick bricklaying. It is worth while building a small wall to get the hang of handling the trowel before you start work on your first project. The bricks can be cleaned off if they have not been laid for more than two hours.

The sequence of scooping up and laying mortar is shown in the adjoining pictures; after a while you will find that this becomes one smooth operation which you carry out automatically.

Professionals use the curved edge of the trowel for cropping (cutting) bricks. You will probably find this difficult to use accurately, so cut bricks with a hammer and bolster and use the trowel only for cleaning up the cut.

1. To pick up mortar, saw off a slice with the trowel, draw it towards you and shape the back of the slice into a curve, with a to-and-fro sawing action.

2. Lift the mortar by sweeping the trowel underneath it from the back. This procedure allows you to load the trowel fully with an easy-to-lay mortar 'sausage'.

3. Do not do this: lifting mortar straight off the heap leaves you with a small, messy load on the trowel, which will probably go everywhere except where you want it.

4. To place the mortar sausage accurately, hold the trowel above the bricks, then pull the trowel back and roll the mortar off it in one smooth action.

5. Smooth the mortar with the trowel point into a bed about 10 mm. ($\frac{3}{8}$ in.) thick. Note the length of the bed, the result of correct picking-up procedure.

6. To form the upright joints between bricks it is best to 'butter' each brick before laying, as here. Buttering a brick already laid may push it out of line.

7. After a brick has been buttered, level off the mortar to about 10 mm. thickness with the V of the trowel. You only need to butter one end of each brick.

8. Finally, trim off the excess mortar around the edges, then lay the brick with the buttered end against the adjoining brick. Check that the joint is 10 mm. thick.

Bricks and bricklaying/5

Using a hammer and bolster

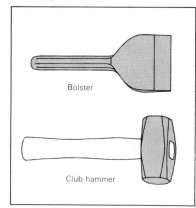

Bolster

Club hammer

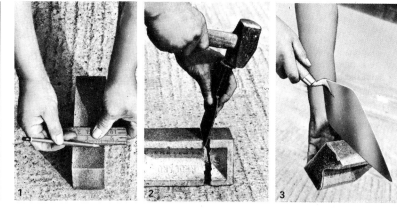

These two tools are used together for cutting bricks while you are working. Buy a hammer of 2 kg. (2–2½ lb.). A bolster is a cold chisel with a 100 mm. (4 in.) wide blade. Cut only sound bricks, as inferior ones shatter when you hit them.

To cut a brick, first mark its face side, where it is to be cut, with a pencil and rule (1). Place the bolster on the pencil line—note the grip (2)—and lean the handle slightly towards the waste part of the brick. Make the cut with a single, sharp blow of the hammer. Tougher bricks may need to be marked and cut from the back as well. Finally, clean up the cut by chopping off irregularities with the trowel if necessary (3). However crooked the cut, the bat is usable if the face side is the right length.

Using a line and pins

A string or nylon line and pins are essential for level bricklaying. The pins have flat blades which are stuck into an upright mortar joint round a corner at each end of the wall. The line is then snagged over a brick at each end and the line stretched tightly between them, just clear of the face of the work, to give a true guide-line against which a course is laid. After you have completed one course this way, move the lines and pins up one course and work similarly.

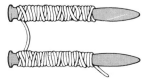

Wind string equally around each pin

An alternative way of working is to make a couple of L-shaped blocks with a groove in them and a screw half driven in on the opposite side. The line can be fitted into the groove, and the blocks clipped on at each end of the wall in the correct position, where they are held by the tension of the line. Wind the spare line around the screw on each block.

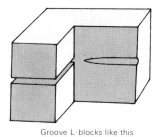

Groove L-blocks like this

If a line breaks, do not knot it together again, as the knot will hold the string away from the brickwork and make it inaccurate. Repair the line by splicing it.

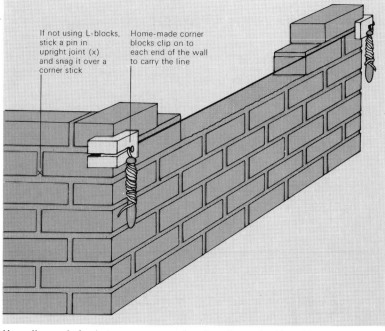

If not using L-blocks, stick a pin in upright joint (x) and snag it over a corner stick

Home-made corner blocks clip on to each end of the wall to carry the line

Use a line and pins between corners and ends, which are always built up first, several courses at a time, and then infilled. The line gives a double guide—to height and to straightness. Lay bricks so that they just touch the line, not push it out.

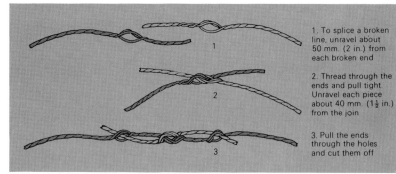

1. To splice a broken line, unravel about 50 mm. (2 in.) from each broken end

2. Thread through the ends and pull tight. Unravel each piece about 40 mm. (1½ in.) from the join

3. Pull the ends through the holes and cut them off

Checking with a spirit level

Use a long spirit level—a 900 mm. (3 ft) one is most easily handled by an amateur—for checking vertical and horizontal work, and for checking 'on the rake'. Hold the level diagonally across the face of the wall, and see if there are any gaps between the level and the brickwork. If there are gaps, the wall is out of true; correct this by gently tapping the bricks back into line against the level.

Always make sure that the bottom of the level is clean—a blob of mortar on one end can give some surprising results.

Testing for accuracy

To check that your spirit level is level, put it on a flat surface which gives a level reading, then turn it sideways through a semicircle and check it again, when it should give the same reading. If it does not, have it adjusted by a tool merchant.

Three-way check: test brickwork for straightness vertically (1), horizontally (2) and on the rake (3 and 4). When checking horizontally or on the rake, the level acts as a straight-edge only—the position of the bubbles has no significance.

Tools you can make yourself

Hawk. For holding a little mortar for pointing and odd mortar-patching jobs. Made from ply, with a handle screwed on.

Large square. For checking corners. Screw together three straight pieces of wood, making a triangle with one side 450 mm. (18 in.), another 600 mm. (2 ft), and the third 750 mm. (2 ft 6 in.) so that the sides are in the ratio 3:4:5. Make a half-joint at the 90° corner and overlap the other two corners

Spot-board. For holding a reserve of mortar. Made from battens and old ply sheet about 600 mm. (2 ft) square

Gauge rod. To ensure that courses are rising evenly. Made from a straight piece of timber with saw marks every 75 mm. (the height of a brick plus the 10 mm. mortar bed)

Bricks and bricklaying/7

Bonding

Any brickwork you do must be bonded—the bricks laid to a pattern, so that the vertical joints in one course do not fall directly above the vertical joints in the course below.

There are structural reasons for this (though the effect is decorative as well): staggered vertical joints mean that downward pressure produced by the dead load of the bricks themselves, and components such as roofs or floor joists, is spread over the wall as a whole.

For practical purposes, only a few of the bricklaying bonds need concern you.

Stretcher bond is the simplest and most widely used bond in modern building. It is used for the minimum 112·5 mm. thick brickwork and for 252·5 mm. thick block used in cavity walls.

English bond and Flemish bond are used for 225 mm. thick and occasional 337·5 mm. thick walls. English bond is stronger, Flemish more decorative.

The alternative English garden wall bond is very popular for 225 mm. thick brickwork because it is almost as strong as Flemish bond but uses fewer of the more expensive facing bricks.

The easiest way of grasping the 'whys and wherefores' of bonding is to practise building walls 'dry', without mortar. You will soon see why bats and closers are needed in every bond to bring about the basic 'staggering' which prevents continuous vertical joints.

The golden rule of all bonding is that the vertical joints should coincide with those in the next course but one.

Stretcher bond consists of identical courses with the long 'stretcher' faces of the bricks laid end-to-end. Joint-staggering is achieved by half-bats at the ends, or by header bricks at the corners.

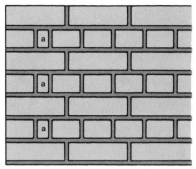

English bond, for 225 mm. thick brickwork. The first course of parallel stretchers is topped by headers laid across the thickness of the wall. Joint-staggering is achieved by queen closers (a).

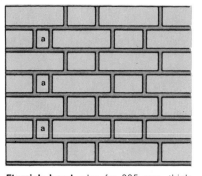

Flemish bond, also for 225 mm. thick brickwork. Courses are identical, consisting of pairs of stretchers laid side by side, alternating with headers. Joints are staggered by queen closers (a).

English garden wall bond, for walls 225 mm. and over, is less strong but less monotonous than English bond. Economical on facing bricks; header courses can be in a different colour from stretcher courses.

Open bonding

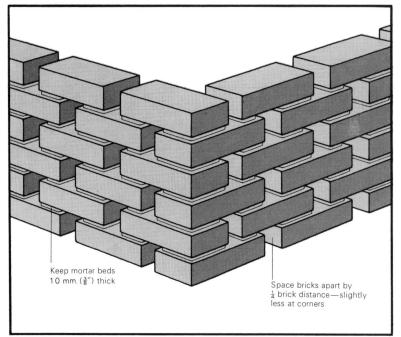

Keep mortar beds 10 mm. (⅜") thick

Space bricks apart by ¼ brick distance—slightly less at corners

Concrete coping

Top-course bricks frog down

Screen walls for gardens and patios can be built economically by using open bond. Lay each course as stretchers separated by quarter-bat spaces. To maintain the bond, slightly reduce spaces on each side of corner bricks.

Finish the top with concrete coping slabs or a solid course of stretcher bricks, frog down, alternating with quarter-bats.

Stretcher bond

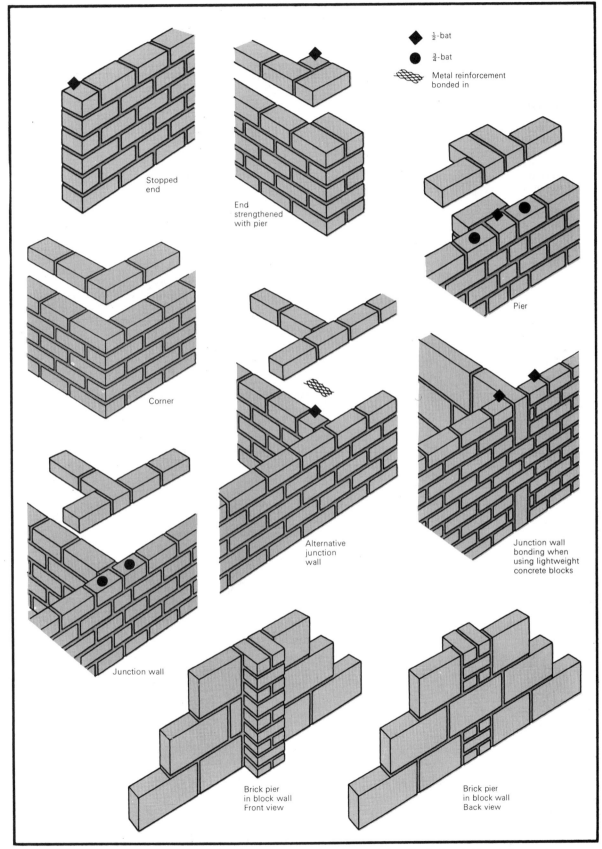

½-bat

¾-bat

Metal reinforcement bonded in

Stopped end

End strengthened with pier

Corner

Pier

Alternative junction wall

Junction wall bonding when using lightweight concrete blocks

Junction wall

Brick pier in block wall Front view

Brick pier in block wall Back view

This page and the next are practical guides to forming ends, corners, junctions and piers. Study them before starting work.

Bricks and bricklaying/9

English bond

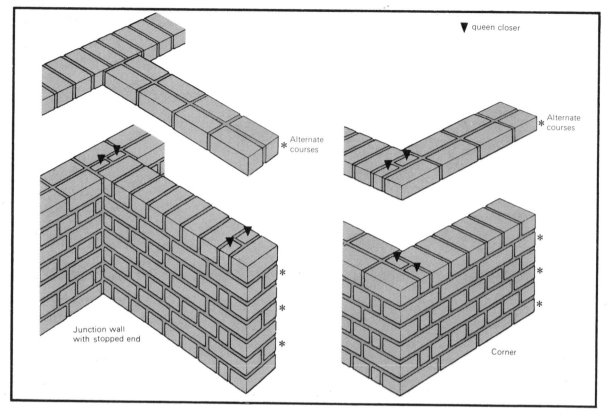

queen closer ▼

Alternate courses *

Alternate courses *

Junction wall with stopped end

Corner

Flemish bond

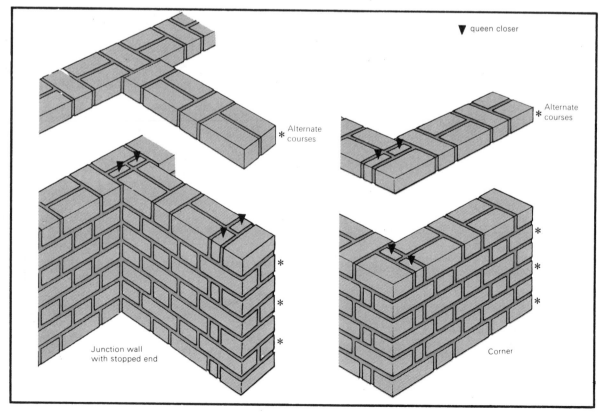

queen closer ▼

Alternate courses *

Alternate courses *

Junction wall with stopped end

Corner

Insulating with cavity walls

Cavity walls, the standard form of construction for buildings to be lived in, consist of two parallel 'leaves' or 'skins' with a gap of 50–100 mm. between them. The still air in the gap acts as a barrier against heat-loss and prevents penetration of damp to the inside of a room's walls.

Weather-resistant facing bricks are used for the external skin. If the cavity is to be filled with insulation, the inner skin can be built with ordinary commons: otherwise it must be of 'thermal' blockwork.

The two skins are held together by wall-ties made either of twisted galvanised steel (fish tail) or wire (butterfly). Ties must be not more than 900 mm. apart in the horizontal or more than 400 mm. apart in the vertical.

Only butterfly wire tails should be used where the inner skin is blockwork.

Fish tail and butterfly wall ties

Mortar or other debris must not be allowed to drop down the cavity during bricklaying, otherwise 'bridges' will be formed, allowing damp to reach and penetrate the inner leaf. To avoid this, lay a batten, with wire loops at each end, over the wall-ties, to trap mortar droppings. When the next course of wall-ties is reached, raise and clean the batten.

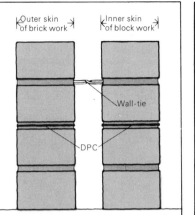

Cut-away view of a cavity wall.

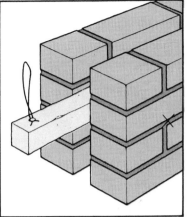

Use a batten to catch mortar droppings.

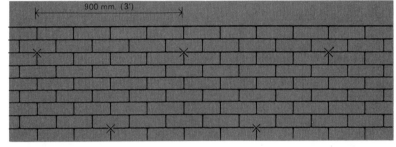

Insert wall-ties between cavity-wall leaves every six courses, in a staggered pattern.

Built-in barriers to rising damp

Bricks in contact with damp earth will draw up moisture as if they were blotting paper, a phenomenon known as 'rising damp'. To prevent this a damp-proof course (DPC) is included in the bedding joint, 150 mm. above soil level.

DPCs, which are required by the building regulations for inhabited buildings, are sold in 112·5, 225 and 337·5 mm. wide rolls, the most convenient for the amateur being made from bituminous felt or black polythene. They are simply rolled on to a 10 mm. (⅜ in.) thick bed of levelled mortar and covered with another mortar bed, after which bricklaying can proceed as usual.

Make sure the bedding mortar is free from sharp stones, which could puncture the material. When reaching the end of one roll and starting on another, overlap both the ends by a generous margin.

DPCs are also advisable for garden walls and non-residential buildings such as workshops and garages.

In house construction, DPCs are required wherever there is a break in the external walls for door or window openings. Concrete sills and lintels are in themselves a damp-proof barrier, but where the gaps in cavity walls are 'stopped' or sealed at the side of a door or window opening, a DPC must be fitted. A typical arrangement is for the DPC to be tucked into a groove in a timber door-frame and then sandwiched between the cavity-closing bricks.

Step the DPC if on a slope, so that it is at least 150 mm. above normal soil level.

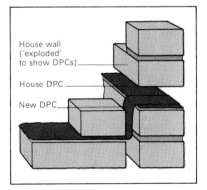

Always overlap joins in DPCs—e.g. when building a garage on to a house.

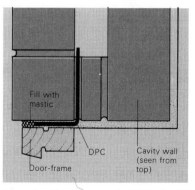

Round a door-frame, the DPC should be wide enough to lap in to the cavity.

Working from a concrete slab

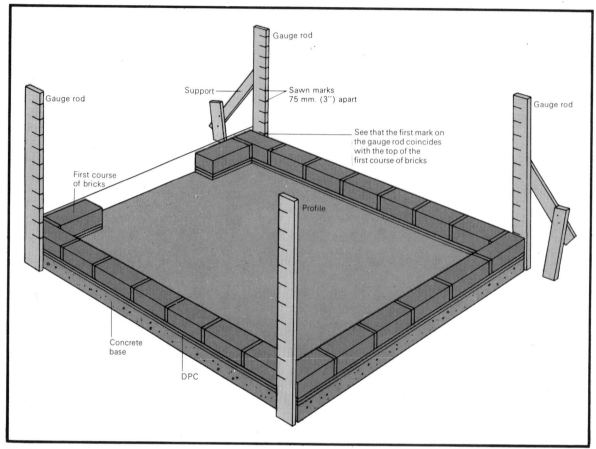

Bricklaying on a concrete base is simple if the slab is level. Lay the first course of bricks on top of a DPC. Set up at each corner a straight length of timber—a profile—marked at 75 mm. intervals. String a line between the marks and lay bricks to it.

The first essential in bricklaying is marking out and building foundations.

For an outbuilding such as a garage or greenhouse, the easiest way of forming a foundation is to construct a level concrete slab for the floor and start bricklaying from it. The procedure for laying a slab is as for laying a concrete drive (see p. 32), but the edge of the slab should be thickened to about 305 mm. to support the weight of the structure.

Make a plan of your building, preferably keeping the length and width to multiples of 112·5 or 225 mm. and the height to multiples of 75 mm.—this keeps brick-cutting on the site down to a minimum. Tailor the dimensions to fit standard-size lintels and door-frames.

Next, check with the local authority about planning permission or Building Regulation approval for the project.

Permission is needed if you are putting up a habitable structure or a garage, and for these you have to submit plans to the planning authority.

Most non-habitable structures can be built in 112·5 mm. thick brickwork, though piers are required at 3 m. intervals and at each end if the walls are more than 3 m. high or 9 m. long. A 230 mm. thick pier would be required at the return to a garage door.

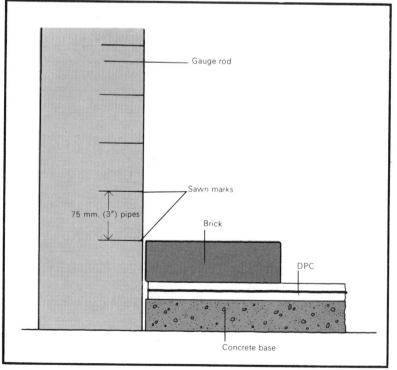

Close-up of a concrete base, with gauge rod and first brick in position.

Setting out strip foundations

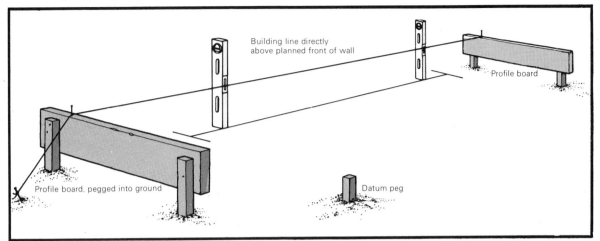

Building line directly above planned front of wall

Profile board

Profile board, pegged into ground

Datum peg

To mark out a concrete strip foundation ('footings') for a wall, set up horizontal profile boards clear of its planned limits, and stretch a line between them, exactly where you want the face of the wall (the building line) to be. Drive a nail into each profile board where the line crosses them, and remove the line. Drive a datum peg into the ground adjoining the site, so that its top is about 150 mm. (6 in.) above normal level. Several vital measurements are made from the datum peg; its top marks the level of the DPC, and irregularities in the brickwork or foundations are made up before you reach DPC level. If there is a danger of the datum peg being disturbed, concrete it into the ground. For concrete work involved in foundations, see p. 14.

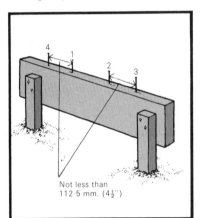

Not less than 112·5 mm. (4½")

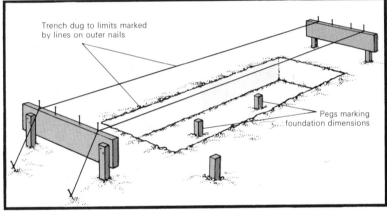

Trench dug to limits marked by lines on outer nails

Pegs marking foundation dimensions

Drive more nails into the profile boards. Nail (1) marks the building line; nail (2) marks the back of the wall and is placed according to the required thickness; nails (3) and (4) mark the width and must be at least 112·5 mm. from the inner nails.

Run lines between the outer nails and dig out the foundation trench between them. Drive pegs into the trench floor so that their tops are multiples of 75 mm. below the top of the datum peg. The tops of these pegs mark the top of the foundations, their length above ground marks the thickness of the foundations. These dimensions vary with local soil conditions, so check the requirements with the building inspector or district surveyor. The trench is now prepared for pouring in concrete.

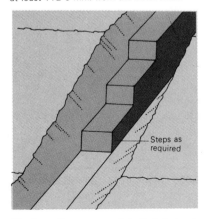

Steps as required

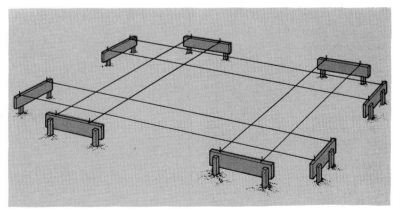

Sloping sites are set out similarly to level ones, except that the foundations are stepped in multiples of 75 mm.—brick height—at convenient intervals.

For more complicated jobs set out strip foundations using the same basic procedure. It is vital to make sure that corners are at right angles. Check this with a square and by measuring diagonals to see that they are identical. Keep the profile boards well back from the planned foundations so that they do not hinder working.

Preparation and procedure

Order all your materials—bricks, sand, cement, DPC rolls, door- and window-frames and lintels—well before you plan to start bricklaying. Have old sacking or polythene sheet to hand for covering work overnight in case of rain or frost.

Choose a mortar mix to suit the type of work, the type of bricks you are using and the weather (see p. 4). Remember that frost is a danger until the mortar is cured and this can take several days.

Do not mix more mortar than you can lay in one working session; two barrow-loads are usually enough. Mix the mortar on a large, dry, clean and level surface such as a sheet of ply or asbestos board. (See p. 31 for how to mix.)

Before starting work, place spot-boards alternately with piles of bricks at 3 m. (10 ft) intervals near the building-line.

Unless the manufacturer has recommended that the bricks should be laid dry, hose them down in hot weather: if they are too dry, they will absorb too much water from the mortar and weaken it.

Keep a bucket of clean water handy for cleaning tools as you work. Mortar dries out your skin, so try not to handle it or, if you do, wear industrial or rubber gloves.

Laying bricks on to a prepared concrete base slab is simply a matter of working accurately between uprights as shown on p. 12. The more normal method—working up from concrete footings—is a little more complicated and is shown in the adjoining step-by-step picture sequence. For the sake of clarity, this has been shown starting from surface level, though footings are always below ground level.

Build up the corners or stopped ends first, taking meticulous care to ensure that they are vertical. The lines and pins are then strung between them and used as a guide to building up the courses in between. Then, if you are building higher, raise the corners or ends again and proceed as before.

1. Stretch strings between uprights to mark the front face of the wall (the building-line). Beneath them, at each corner or stopped end, lay a thin layer (screed) of mortar. This is used for marking out guide lines for laying bricks.

2. Hold the spirit level against the string—taking care not to bend it—and steady the level upright with a batten. Where the foot of the level touches the screed, scratch a mark with the front of the trowel—the mark should be directly under the string.

3. Repeat this procedure, making another mark for the same line about 600 mm. (2 ft) away from the first. Join up the two marks, using a straight-edge, to form line (A). Now mark line (B) at right angles to line (A). Repeat this at all corners or stopped ends. You will now have transferred the building-line from the strings to the mortar screeds. Take plenty of time over this operation—if it is wrong, all later work will be out of line. Once you have done it, remove the strings ready for actual bricklaying.

4. Lay a 9–10 mm. ($\frac{3}{8}$ in.) mortar bed at one corner or end, taking care not to cover up the scored lines. Very carefully, lay the corner brick and level it against the lines—this first brick sets the line for later brickwork which should be checked against it.

5. Lay six or so bricks along both arms of the corner, still keeping to the marked lines and checking against the corner brick with the level. Check the width of cross-joints—they should be 9–10 mm. thick. Build up the corner to the second course above base level. This course is laid with the bricks frog down, to provide a level base for the DPC. Inaccuracies in the foundations must be 'taken up' in the brickwork by the time you reach DPC level, so that from then on you are building absolutely level.

6. Lay a thin mortar bed for the DPC and roll it out from the corner in each direction, overlapping the ends. Smooth the DPC flat with the trowel, taking care not to puncture it. Cover the DPC with a mortar bed and continue laying bricks above it.

7. As you continue laying bricks, form the cross-joints as you go by wiping a dab of mortar on one end of the brick, spreading it all over the end and trimming it to size—only one end of the brick needs to be buttered in this way.

8. Use the point of the trowel to make sure that the mortar is spread evenly all over the end of the brick. You may see professionals buttering on the cross-joints after laying the brick; doing it before avoids the chance of moving the brick out of line.

9. After the DPC is laid, take the corner or end up for several courses and use the gauge-rod after the DPC, to ensure that courses rise evenly. Every line on the gauge-rod should coincide with the top of a brick. 'Rack back' the corner or end as you build up, forming a step pattern.

10. Use the spirit level as well as the gauge-rod to check for accuracy at this stage. Check the work vertically, horizontally and on the rake, holding the level diagonally across the wall from the corner brick and gently tapping back any bricks which are out of line. After completing one corner or end, start work on the others, taking each up to the same height. Then string a line between them and fill in the courses, working to the line. When you have done this, build up the corners or ends again and continue infilling until you reach the required height.

11. Inside view of the base of a corner—it can be left rough if it will not show or if it is to be rendered over. Take care, however, to keep the face side clean and free of mortar droppings—wipe these off before they harden, as they are difficult to remove later.

12. Before the mortar hardens it must be pointed—made neat and weather-resistant. To form a rubbed joint, use a rounded length of metal, such as the handle of an old galvanised bucket. Rub it up and down the cross-joints first, to form a slight hollow.

13. Next rub the horizontal joints, and finally brush off excess mortar. The rubbed joint is fairly quick and simple. For details of how to form others (such as flush, recessed or weather-struck joints), see Re-pointing brickwork, pp. 43–44.

Decorative arch

Building a load-bearing arch is beyond the scope of the amateur. A decorative arch is not difficult, however.

Use a length of black mild steel, bent to shape, as a support for the brickwork. If the wall is 112·5 mm. thick, use a piece of steel 50 mm. (2 in.) wide and 9 mm. (⅜ in.) thick; for a 225 mm. thick wall, use a piece 150 mm. (6 in.) wide. Bond it in place in the side walls, then build up the brickwork. Use standard bricks on end with wedge-shaped mortar beds between them. The side walls can be carried up and over the arch, or the arch can be finished with a weatherproof bed of mortar on top. Fix door- and window-frames to brickwork with galvanised frame cramps, screwed into the frame and bedded into the mortar. Use a board and bricks to keep frames upright. When you build up to the top of the frame, mortar in the lintel. Lintels must overlap the frame 150 mm. (6 in.) each side for window- and door-frames.

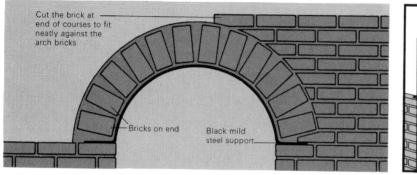
Cut the brick at end of courses to fit neatly against the arch bricks

Bricks on end

Black mild steel support

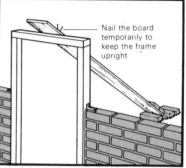
Nail the board temporarily to keep the frame upright

Roofing

A felt and granite-chip roof is suitable for lean-to brick structures.

Lay a course of cut bricks (1) on the top of each end wall to form a slight slope.

Bed 100 × 50 mm. wooden wall plates (2) on a 12 mm. (½ in.) mortar bed on top of each wall. Fix a 100 × 50 mm. plate to the existing house wall with rag bolts, its underside level with the undersides of the adjoining wall plates.

Nail 100 × 50 mm. rafters (3) approximately 400 mm. (16 in.) apart between the side wall plate and the house wall plate, half-lapping them on to the house wall plate. Fix the first half-way between the end wall plates and work out from it.

Nail 100 × 50 mm. noggings (4) at 600 mm. (2 ft) maximum centres between the rafters. Nail the end rafters to the projecting noggings, leaving the rafters just overlapping the structure.

Nail the fascia board (5) to the projecting ends of the rafters. Nail rectangular end pieces (6) to the end of the rafter overhang to give a level fixing for the soffit (7), fix the fascia board and then the soffits.

Cover the whole roof skeleton with 20 mm. flaxboard (8); fix edging battens (9). Clout-nail the first felt layer, bond on the second layer of felt with brush-on bituminous-based liquid, fix the mineral felt drips to the edges and bond the third and final felt layer. Overlap the joints in the felt; make sure joints in each layer do not coincide. Scatter granite chips over the top layer after coating with bitumen.

Seal the joint between the roof and house with a flashing of mineral felt mortared in the house wall and stuck on to the felt.

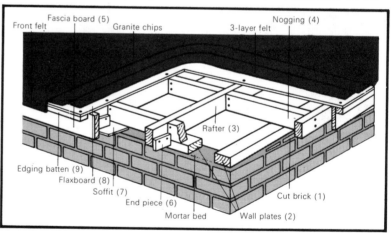
Fascia board (5)
Front felt
Granite chips
Nogging (4)
3-layer felt
Rafter (3)
Edging batten (9)
Flaxboard (8)
Soffit (7)
End piece (6)
Mortar bed
Cut brick (1)
Wall plates (2)

Lean-to roof structure. Nail through noggings diagonally into rafters.

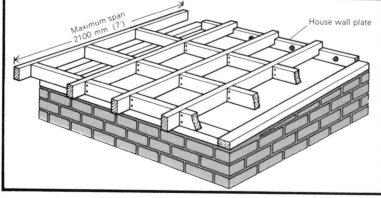
Maximum span 2100 mm. (7')
House wall plate

Layout of rafters. Note how the end rafter slightly overhangs the structure.

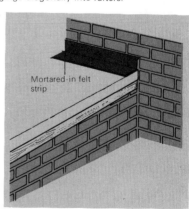
Mortared-in felt strip

Fitting flashing into a house wall.

Spanning openings above door and window frames

Brickwork above a door or window frame must be supported by a lintel, which may be either of reinforced concrete or of galvanised steel. Both types are made to span openings in 112·5 mm. and 225 mm. solid walls and in 337·5 mm. cavity walls. Lintels will be needed for such jobs as building a brick garage, outhouse or kitchen extension. They can be bought from builders' merchants.

Since concrete lintels of all but the smallest sizes are very heavy, do not attempt to fit one without help and then not unless you and your helper can, each on his own, lift the lintel without undue strain. To allow a proper margin of safety, work from a stoutly built platform or from scaffolding, with two thicknesses of

scaffold boards so that you do not need to lift the lintel above waist height. If this is not practicable, then the job is best left to a builder.

A concrete lintel is visible unless the brickwork of the wall is rendered, in which case the face and the underside of the lintel should also be rendered.

A steel lintel has the advantage of not showing on the face of the brickwork, and is also much lighter than a concrete one. Two types of steel lintel are manufactured for use in cavity walls. The Standard lintel cannot be used alone but must be supported by a concrete lintel on the inner wall of the cavity. The Combined type is more complex in design and supports both the inner and the outer wall.

Buy a lintel at least 300 mm. (1 ft) longer than the gap to be spanned, for at least 150 mm. of it at either end needs to rest on the supporting surface.

All lintels must have a bearing of not less than 150 mm. (6 in.) at each end. Bed the lintel on to mortar so that its weight is borne entirely by the brickwork: at no point should it rest on a door or window frame.

If the top of the frame does not line up with the top of the bricks in a course, build up the frame with wood to the level of the bricks only.

Finally, squeeze a mastic sealer into the space between the lintel and the top of the frame; the mastic will remain flexible and will not harden or crack.

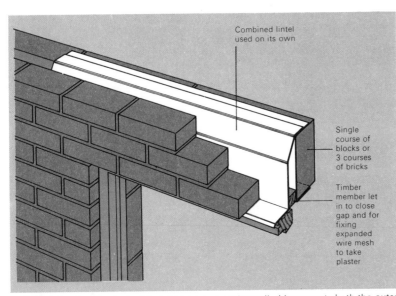

Combined galvanised steel lintel Used on a cavity wall, this supports both the outer and the inner walls. Note the uninterrupted brickwork above door or window frame.

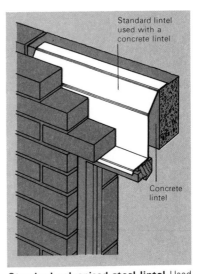

Standard galvanised steel lintel Used also on a cavity wall, this holds only the outer skin of the wall; the inner wall is supported by a reinforced concrete lintel.

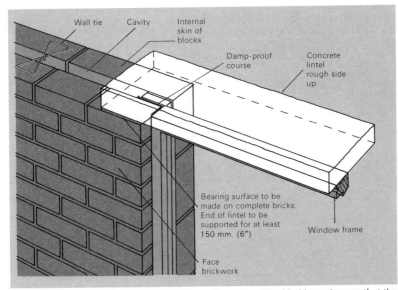

Pre-stressed concrete lintel Used on a cavity wall and bedded into place so that the face of the lintel is flush with the brickwork. Make sure that the bearing surface is laid on complete bricks and that both ends of the lintel are supported for at least 150 mm. (6 in.).

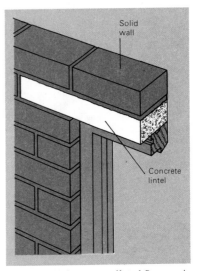

Pre-stressed concrete lintel Commonly used above door frames or hatchways on solid internal walls. Some authorities insist on a minimum of three courses of brick above such lintels.

Rendering walls

With care, and a fair amount of practice at rendering small areas, a handyman can produce a first-class finish. Scaffolding is essential to reach all parts of the wall comfortably. This is not a ladder job.

You need a steel float for a smooth finish, a wooden float for a more matt finish, a hawk, a mortar board (with a stand if possible), a straight-edged board about 2 m. (7 ft) long, and pieces of timber 10 mm. (⅜ in.) thick as screeds.

You can make a hawk from a piece of exterior-grade plywood about 300 mm. (12 in.) square, with a short length of broom handle fitted to the centre.

The mortar board should be about 675 mm. (2 ft 3 in.) square, and the stand about 750 mm. (2 ft 6 in.) high. You can make the board from tongued and grooved boards.

The 10 mm. thickness of the battens corresponds to the depth of the first coat of rendering. Hack off all loose material, rake out pointing to a depth of about 10 mm.

(⅜ in.), then wire-brush the wall to remove loose dust and dirt.

Nail the first timber batten to the wall at a corner with masonry nails, using a builder's level to ensure the batten is up-right. Knock the nails into the mortar joints, flush with the batten.

Space further screeds at distances of 1500 mm. (5 ft), so that you have a row of vertical pieces of timber with working bays between them. Each of these bays will be filled individually.

Making the mix

Only mix at one time as much mortar as you can handle in about half an hour—less if the weather is hot.

You need sand that has not too much loam in it: a mixture of soft sand and sharp sand is best. Ask a builders' merchant for a good sand, explaining what it is for.

Make a mix of 1 part of cement to 4 of sand by volume. As a guide, 350 kg. of cement and 1 cu. m. of sand will cover about 20 sq. m. (20–25 sq. yds) of wall.

Concrete block walls need a weaker mix than brick walls. A 1:2:9 mix of cement,

lime and sand is good for most purposes, but a 1:1:6 mix may be needed in winter or on a severely exposed wall.

Tip, say, four buckets of sand on to a clean, dry surface and add a bucket of cement. As you become used to the job, you will be able to increase these quantities to suit your working speed.

Mix well until the colour is even, then make a hole in the centre of the heap and add water.

To improve adhesion and make the mix smoother, you can add a PVA liquid to the

water. Your builders' merchant should be able to supply this, and the instructions will tell you how much to use.

Do not add too much water. The mix should be pliable, yet firm enough not to slide off the hawk, and there should be no dry patches in it.

It is a good idea to record the exact amount of water used in the first batch, then you will be able to repeat the mix or vary the water content as necessary.

Spreading the mix

Place two buckets of mortar on the board and, if the wall is dry, flick water on to it with a brush to dampen it.

Holding the hawk flush with the top of the board, scrape on to it several floatfuls of mortar.

Hold the hawk near the bottom of the first bay. Now the action is to cut away a section of the mortar, tip the hawk and scrape the mortar on to the float, holding the float almost upside-down.

Push mortar from the float on to the wall and spread it from the bottom up-wards.

It is a good idea to have a row of boards along the foot of the wall to collect mortar droppings. Do not worry about what you drop: simply gather it up and use it again.

Continue filling in between the two screeds until mortar is just higher than their surfaces. Then skim off excess mortar with the straight-edge, resting it on the two screeds and using it in a see-saw action.

If any hollows show up, fill them with mortar and repeat the skimming until you have a flat surface.

Carry on applying, mixing and levelling until a whole bay is finished; then start on a second section of wall, leaving all screeds in position.

When the mortar has had three or four hours in which to set, scratch the surface in a random pattern to produce a key for the next coat.

You can make a scratcher by knocking a row of nails through a piece of wood.

Remove the screeds, fill the gaps with mortar and level off.

Allow the mortar 24 hours to set, then dampen and apply a second, thinner coat.

Use a wood float for a matt finish, and

a steel float for a really smooth finish, but do not over-trowel or you will bring the cement to the surface of the rendering.

Use wide, sweeping strokes with the float, taking down all irregularities.

Another way of getting rendering on to a wall is to hire a special tool called a Tyrolean Projector. As you turn a side handle, sprung prongs on the projector fling the mix on to the wall with considerable force.

This method gives an attractive coating which is ideal for hiding irregularities.

Special finishes

You can texture the final coat of rendering by dabbing it with a ball of newspaper or by using a decorator's comb.

To give a granular finish, fling pebbles

or spar on to the wet top coat from a small shovel. Lay sacking at the wall base, to collect stones which do not stick.

Re-rendering

Walls already rendered but in poor condition can be re-rendered. Chip away the old rendering and start from bare brick. Use a bonding fluid, so that the new rendering gets a good grip.

Cleaning up

Be sure to clean all your tools thoroughly after use. Mortar washes off easily when wet, but once set it is very hard to remove. Protect paths, tiled roofs over bays, and plants against mortar droppings. Polythene dust sheeting is useful because it can be hosed down.

Applying the first coat of mortar.

Finishing smoothly, using a steel float.

Paving and paths

The exposed aggregate slabs are relieved by broad joints of coloured mortar and regularly spaced brick courses.

Hexagonal slabs in contrasting colours.

Stepping-stones can save wear on a lawn.

Decorative grooves drain concrete.

Projects/2

Types of paving

Concrete

When laid *in situ* it makes a strong, functional surface for areas around the house; as a garden path it tends to look dull and severe. For added interest cut grooves in the surface, to simulate crazy paving, about an hour after laying the concrete.

For a cobbled effect, set pebbles upright in a mortar bed to a little more than half their depth. Do not leave spaces between the pebbles. If the path is to be used for a mower or barrow, use the pebbles as an edging only.

Pre-cast concrete slabs

These allow greater variation and have a more professional appearance. They are sold in a variety of colours and shapes, some with surfaces resembling natural stone. Simple designs and muted colours are the most effective.

Crazy paving

Made from natural stone or broken concrete slabs, it has an informal appearance in keeping with most settings. Pieces 250 mm. (9 in.) or more across look best, with borders formed from large pieces having one fairly straight edge. For a lasting, weed-free path, lay the stones on a mortar bed and fill the joints with mortar. Avoid symmetrical patterns, large areas of mortar and continuous straight joints.

Natural stone paving

This is laid in the same way as concrete slabs and has a mellow, mature quality. Some types are expensive, especially if transported a long way from the quarry. Stone slabs and cobbles go well together —the latter helping to reduce costs—and provide scope for individuality in the design of paths and terraces.

Brick

Brick paths are unobtrusive and free-draining, but avoid soft types, such as internal flettons, which crumble in frost. For an extra-strong path, set the bricks in a bed of mortar; otherwise bed them in a 25 mm. (1 in.) layer of sand or ashes, with only the tops protruding above ground level. To cover 1 sq. m., 39 bricks laid flat are needed or 59 on edge.

The random slabs of old London stone are edged with a concrete kerb.

A distinctive walk made with facing bricks laid flat in a squared pattern.

Cobbled paving, laid *in situ*.

A herringbone design on a sand base.

A coursed brick patio with mortared joints.

Steps

Garden steps offer considerable scope for originality. They can be straight or curving, inset or protruding, abrupt or gradual. Brick, stone, concrete slabs and broken paving are among the most suitable construction materials.

Design your steps on generous lines; narrow flights with shallow treads seldom look right in a garden setting. On gently sloping ground, the treads can be as deep as you wish and the risers only an inch or two high; on a steep bank do not make the risers more than 175 mm. (7 in.) high or the treads less than 280 mm. (11 in.) deep.

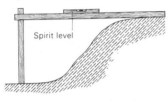

Measuring the overall height of a slope.

To determine the size and number of steps needed, first measure the difference in height between the top and bottom of the slope, dividing this into equal units of not more than 175 mm. Then decide on a suitable depth for the treads, if necessary broadening the contour of the slope by extending the base with soil dug from the top.

Treads and risers are of old London stone.

Edged by ivy and a hosta, these home-cast slabs have a weathered, mature appearance.

Exposed flints relieve the concrete risers.

The hard lines of sawn Portland stone are obscured by container-grown plants.

Projects/4
Walls

A dry wall of Cotswold stone, planted with thyme, thrift, heather and a dwarf broom.

Granite makes an attractive, durable wall.

A composite wall of brick, stone and tile.

This stepped raised bed was built with cemented York stone blocks and slabs.

Types of walls

Low walls, constructed of brick or stone, are useful as edgings for terraces, for supporting banks and for making raised flower beds. Get professional advice about the construction of retaining walls more than 1220 mm. (4 ft) high.

There are two quite different forms of construction—dry and cemented.

No mortar is needed for dry walls, which are mostly built with natural stone. For the traditional type of agricultural dry stone wall, each course is laid directly on the one beneath. In gardens, the stones are generally bedded in soil, with plants set at random at the foot of vertical joints.

If the soil is on the heavy side, mix some sharp sand with it before packing the joints. Also add bone-meal, at the rate of about 3 grams per litre (4 oz. per bushel), to give the plants a good start during their first growing season.

Dry walls take less time to construct than cemented walls and have a pleasingly informal appearance. Build them with a slight backwards slope—75–100 mm. (3–4 in.) for a 900 mm. (3 ft) wall—with longer tie stones set every 1000–1500 mm. (4–5 ft) for greater stability.

For cemented walls use natural or reconstructed stone blocks—laying irregular courses if you prefer an informal appearance—or weathered bricks. For a colourful effect, build a double wall, making drainage holes in the foundations and filling the cavity with good loam. Place stones or small rubble, topped with shingle, at the bottom of the cavity, and set plants along the top. Add bone-meal at the rate of about

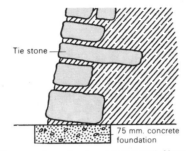

Planting positions in a dry wall. Bond the courses to avoid straight vertical joints; firm the soil thoroughly. A backwards slope directs water to the plants' roots.

Cross-section of a dry retaining wall. Note how the stones are set at an angle, with a tie stone half-way up. Give foundations to dry walls more than 900 mm. (3 ft) high.

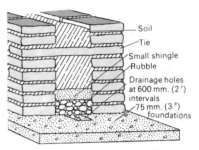

Build raised beds with either dry or cemented walls. Leave drainage gaps in the bottom course of cemented walls if built on paving; lay rubble over the base.

Set tie stones or metal rods every 1800 mm. (6 ft) in a hollow wall. Use timber plugs to form drain holes in the footings, removing them as the concrete hardens.

3 grams per litre (4 oz. per bushel) to the top 150 mm. (6 in.) in the cavity.

Concrete foundations are essential for cemented walls and advisable for dry walls more than 900 mm. (3 ft) high. Leave 'weep holes' (gaps for drainage) in the bottom course of cemented retaining walls, to prevent waterlogging.

Plants for dry walls

Alyssum saxatile (yellow, April–June);
Aubrieta deltoidea (purple, April–June);
Dianthus alpinus (pink to red, June);
Dryas octopetala (white, June–July);
Erinus alpinus (pink, March–August);
Leontopodium alpinum (creamy yellow, May–July).

Painted brickwork brightens a shady patio.

Spiral wall built with multi-coloured stocks.

Designer: John Brookes

The plastic mesh will encourage the ivy to spread over this wall of reconstructed stone.

Projects/6
Settings for plants

A well-proportioned pergola, with tile and York stone uprights, covered with vigorous rambler roses.

An open-bonded brick screen is an excellent support for climbing plants.

This stone sink garden provides a natural setting for alpines. It is important to fill sinks with free-draining compost.

Brick barbecue

A large functional barbecue built on a concrete slab foundation with surrounding brick paving.

Projects/8

Garden pools

A simple fountain adds interest to this formal patio pool.

A rock cascade in a natural setting.

Paving slabs used with pebbles and rocks for a terrace pool.

Jobs you can do with concrete

Concrete is a versatile and relatively cheap building material. Once you have learnt the basic technique of handling it, you can use it to carry out a whole range of improvements.

For do-it-yourself purposes, concrete has two forms—*in situ* and pre-cast.

In situ concrete is poured on to a prepared base directly after mixing, then tamped and levelled. It is used for paths, drives, foundations and bases for structures such as garages and sheds. You can mix it yourself, by hand or machine, or order ready-mixed concrete, which is delivered, ready for pouring, by a lorry.

Pre-cast concrete is ready-made paving slabs or walling blocks which are bedded down or bonded together with mortar. You can cast your own slabs and blocks or buy them ready-made in a wide range of patterns and colours. Factory-made units are made to standards which cannot be matched by do-it-yourself methods.

Concrete consists basically of only three ingredients: cement, water and aggregate (stones and sand in controlled quantities).

Mortar consists of the same ingredients, except that the aggregate has no stones in it. It is used as rendering, to provide a waterproof skin for bricks and blockwork, as well as for bedding and jointing. Grout is a runny mortar used for repairs.

Careful mixing of the ingredients is vital for good results. It pays to have an understanding of the part played by each in producing a good mix.

Two pairs of hands make lighter work of concreting. If your wife will help, she can take care of levelling and compaction while you see to mixing and barrowing.

Choosing the correct ingredients

Cement. The ordinary Portland cement—which is what you get when you ask for cement at a builders' merchant—will cope with most jobs. It is the familiar grey powder sold under various brand names and is normally supplied in 50 kg. bags, though smaller quantities are available from do-it-yourself shops. It is called 'Portland' because concrete made with it resembles Portland stone.

There are also several special cements for particular purposes.

White Portland cement can look attractive when used with coloured slabs and for rendering.

Pigments used to obtain other colours need careful and thorough mixing for consistency. It is generally better to use special coloured sand or chippings, which result in a more natural colour than can be obtained with pigments.

Masonry cement, which has a slower setting time, helps in brick or block-laying.

Rapid-hardening cement may be useful if concreting has to be carried out in cold weather.

Water combines with the cement to form a stone-like 'mineral glue', which binds the particles of aggregate and gives concrete and mortar their bonding power.

Use as little water as possible. Only a fraction of the water in the mix is used up in the chemical reaction that hardens the concrete. The remaining water has to escape by evaporation, leaving minute voids that weaken the concrete.

In theory, the ideal mix would contain only 1 part of water (by weight) for every 4 parts of cement. All the water would be absorbed in hardening and none left to evaporate. In practice, such a mix would be too stiff to use.

The moisture content of the aggregate varies, so it is impossible to state just how much water should be added. However, you will get satisfactory results if you add just enough for a workable mix.

Use tap or spring water; river water often contains impurities which affect setting, while sea water may leave a white deposit on the surface.

Aggregate gives bulk and strength to concrete. It consists of fine (up to 4·76 mm. dia.) and coarse particles.

The correct ratio of fine particles (sand) to coarse is vital for good concrete; ideally, they should be measured out separately according to the type of mix you are using. However, for do-it-yourself jobs you can save work by telling the supplier the nature of the job and asking for a suitable all-in aggregate.

In some parts of the country this will consist of washed ballast; in others, of reconstituted all-in aggregate, made up at the plant in correct proportions to suit the job in hand.

Both types must be mixed to an even consistency before use.

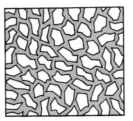 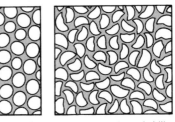

Types of aggregate. Crushed stone (left) has sharp, angular particles which interlock to give strength but produce a hard-to-work mix. In natural, uncrushed river gravel or sand (centre) the smooth, rounded particles give good workability but less strength. Crushed gravel (right) combines smooth and angular particles, giving a mix of medium strength and fair workability.

Concrete and cement/2

How to store raw materials

Do not buy cement until just before you want to use it—under average conditions it may start to deteriorate and go hard in 7-14 days. To keep contact with damp to a minimum, store bags of cement clear of the ground in a dry place, stacking the bags tightly and keeping them away from possible contamination from other materials, such as plaster, lime or other types of cement.

Store sand and stones, if purchased separately, in individual heaps on a clean, hard surface.

Keep them well away from each other to prevent them from becoming mixed. Cover the piles with polythene sheeting if they are in the open.

Make sure that aggregates are not dumped on top of drains or gullies, which will become blocked.

If dumped outside the house they must not obstruct the pavement and should be barrowed in from the roadside as quickly as possible.

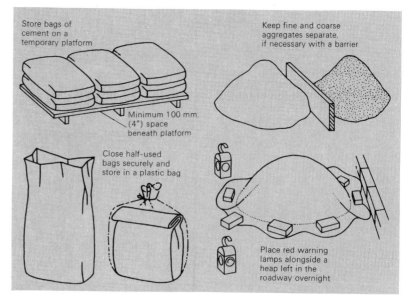

Store bags of cement on a temporary platform

Keep fine and coarse aggregates separate, if necessary with a barrier

Minimum 100 mm. (4") space beneath platform

Close half-used bags securely and store in a plastic bag

Place red warning lamps alongside a heap left in the roadway overnight

Tools and equipment for concreting

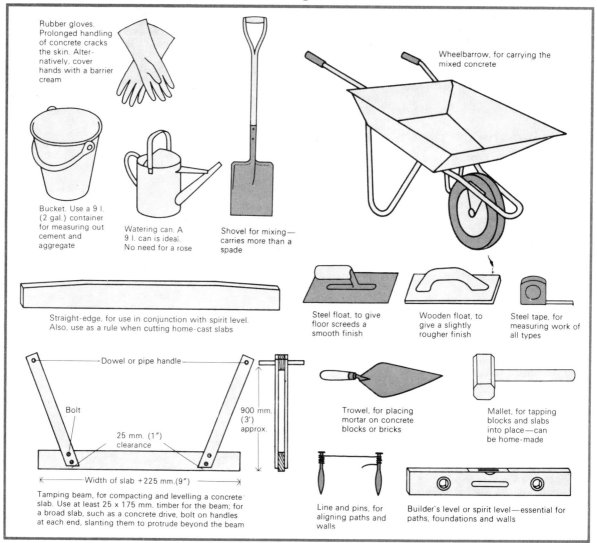

Rubber gloves. Prolonged handling of concrete cracks the skin. Alternatively, cover hands with a barrier cream

Wheelbarrow, for carrying the mixed concrete

Bucket. Use a 9 l. (2 gal.) container for measuring out cement and aggregate

Watering can. A 9 l. can is ideal. No need for a rose

Shovel for mixing—carries more than a spade

Straight-edge, for use in conjunction with spirit level. Also, use as a rule when cutting home-cast slabs

Steel float, to give floor screeds a smooth finish

Wooden float, to give a slightly rougher finish

Steel tape, for measuring work of all types

Dowel or pipe handle

Bolt

900 mm. (3') approx.

25 mm. (1") clearance

Width of slab +225 mm.(9")

Tamping beam, for compacting and levelling a concrete slab. Use at least 25 x 175 mm. timber for the beam; for a broad slab, such as a concrete drive, bolt on handles at each end, slanting them to protrude beyond the beam

Trowel, for placing mortar on concrete blocks or bricks

Mallet, for tapping blocks and slabs into place—can be home-made

Line and pins, for aligning paths and walls

Builder's level or spirit level—essential for paths, foundations and walls

1. Work out the area to be covered

Whether you plan to use ready-mixed concrete or to mix your own, the first thing you need to know is 'how much'. Work this out in four simple stages:

First, calculate the area to be covered, as shown in the diagrams (right).

Second, determine the volume of concrete needed.

Third, decide on the correct mix.

Fourth, calculate the quantities of cement and all-in aggregate (or cement, sand and coarse aggregate) required.

All-in aggregate is particularly useful for small jobs, as separate ingredients may be unobtainable in quantities of less than ½ cu. m. It is better to err on the generous side when ordering.

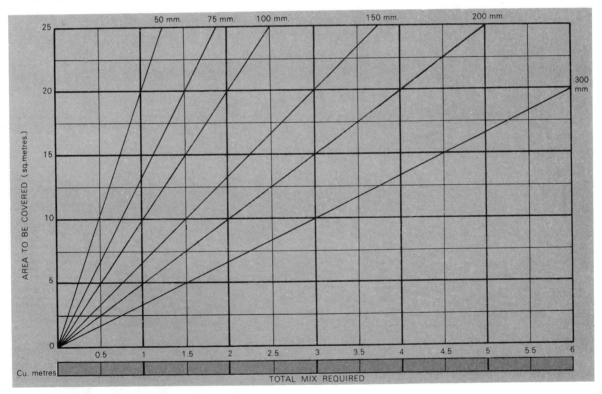

To calculate the area of a rectangle, multiply the length by the width

To find the area of a circle, multiply the square of the radius by 3.1416

The area of a triangle is found by multiplying half the length of the base by the perpendicular height

Estimate complex areas by sketching them on squared paper. Count up whole squares and those that are more than one-third filled

2. Work out how much concrete you need

Use this table to calculate the total mix required. Read across from the area scale on the left of the table to the line for the thickness of concrete, and then down to the total quantity scale, to obtain the required number of cu. metres of mix that will be needed for the work planned.

For example, an area of 20 sq. m. to be covered with a 75 mm. slab will require about 1·8 cu. m.; 22 sq. m. covered by a 100 mm. slab will need about 2.3 cu. m.

Thicknesses not given in the table can be calculated by addition—e.g., for a 125 mm. slab, add together the amounts needed for 50 and 75 mm. slabs.

3. Choose your mix

For almost all do-it-yourself concreting, one of three mixes will be suitable. Use separate aggregates when quantities needed can be obtained economically.

If you propose using an all-in aggregate, your supplier will advise you about the suitability of local as-dug ballast.

If it is not suitable, order reconstituted all-in aggregate, or order stones and sand separately and mix them yourself.

Ready-mixed concrete is not usually economical for less than 3 cu. m.

Mix A. A general purpose mix suitable for foundations, drives, floor slabs and other heavy-duty work.
1 part cement
5 parts all-in aggregate (max. size of 20 mm.)
or
1 part cement
2½ parts sand
4 parts coarse aggregate (max. 20 mm.)
If ordering ready-mixed concrete, the equivalent mix is C20P.

Mix B. For paths and thin sections.
1 part cement
3¾ parts all-in aggregate (10 mm. max.)
or
1 part cement
2 parts sand
3 parts coarse aggregate (10 mm. max.).
Mix C. For paving less than 50 mm. thick and bedding mortar for slabs and step treads:
1 part cement
3 parts coarse sand

4. How much cement? How much aggregate?

When you have decided on the mix and calculated the total volume of concrete required, read off from this table how much you need of each ingredient.

First read along the top to find the quantity of mix required. Then follow the nearest line downward to find the number of bags of cement and the quantities of sand and coarse aggregate, or of all-in aggregate, needed for that particular quantity of mix.

Unless the line passes exactly through a quantity mark, always read the figure on the right of the line: it is better to over-order than to under-order and find that you have exhausted your concrete before completing the work in hand.

Though aggregate quantities are given in quarter multiples of cu. metres (to help calculate larger quantities), few merchants will deliver less than ½ cu. m. without an additional charge—which would make the purchase uneconomical.

Example: to make 2·2 cu. m. of Mix A, order 12 bags of cement and either 1 cu. m. of sand and 1·75 cu. m. of coarse aggregate or 2 cu. m. all-in aggregate.

CONCRETE REQUIRED Cu. metres		Scale: 0.5 · 1 · 1.5 · 2 · 2.5
MIX A	Cement (50 kg. bags)	1 2 3 4 5 6 7 8 9 10 11 12 13
	Sand (cu. m.)	0.25 0.5 0.75 1
	Coarse aggregate (cu. m.)	0.25 0.5 0.75 1 1.25 1.5 1.75
	All-in aggregate (cu. m.) (1:5 mix)	0.25 0.5 0.75 1 1.25 1.5 1.75
MIX B	Cement (50 kg. bags)	1 2 3 4 5 6 7 8 9 10 11 12 13 14 15 16 17
	Sand (cu.m.)	0.25 0.5 0.75 1
	Coarse aggregate (cu. m.)	0.25 0.5 0.75 1 1.25 1.5 1.75
	All-in aggregate (cu.m.) (1:3½ mix)	0.25 0.5 0.75 1 1.25 1.5 1.75 2
MIX C	Cement (50 kg. bags)	1 2 3 4 5 6 7 8 9 10 11 12 13 14 15 16 17 18 19 20 21 22 23 24 25
	Sand (cu.m.)	0.25 0.5 0.75 1 1.25 1.5 1.75 2 2.25 2.5 2.75 3

When to buy ready-mixed concrete

Once you have found how much concrete you want, decide whether it is worth ordering and mixing the separate ingredients yourself or whether you can save trouble by ordering ready-mixed concrete.

For areas needing more than 3 cu. m. of concrete, it is usually better to buy ready-mixed concrete—wet, freshly mixed concrete delivered by truck.

The cost of ready-mixed concrete compares favourably with concrete mixed at home. As a rough guide, ready-mixed concrete in loads of 3 cu. m. or more costs about £13·50 per cu. m., plus a delivery charge based on mileage. Under 3 cu. m., the cost per cu. m. rises fairly steeply. When ordering, say what job you want the concrete for, and how much.

If the area to be covered is small, save time and trouble by buying bags of dry-mixed concrete.

Dry-mixed concrete, such as Marley-mix, is sold in large bags containing enough to cover about 0·025 cu. m. (0·9 cu. ft.). Hardware and do-it-yourself shops also sell smaller bags from about 3 kg. (7 lb.) upwards.

Dry-mixed concrete saves storing, batching and mixing the separate ingredients; all you do is add the water. It is especially useful for jobs where space is limited. However, it is more expensive than if you mix the ingredients yourself.

Handling ready-mixed concrete. The site must be fully prepared, with all formwork in place, when the lorry arrives. Provide planks for the lorry to back up on if there is no hard standing for it. If the load cannot be poured direct into the prepared formwork, have a barrow handy to transport it. But moving a delivery of ready-mixed concrete is not a job that can be done single-handed. It should be borne in mind that the concrete must be laid within about two hours of its delivery, and that 1 cu. m. weighs about 2·4 tonnes (2·36 tons), or about 40 barrow-loads.

How to mix by hand

Materials and tools. Measure out the aggregates, whether separate (as here) or all-in, by filling the bucket and levelling off with the shovel. Measure cement in the same way, shaking it well down in the bucket and scraping off level.

Dump the cement on top of the aggregate and mix until the colour is even. (With separate aggregates, mix the cement and sand, then add the stones.) Turn the mix over, forming a new heap, at least three times, shovelling from the base.

Form a crater in the middle of the heap, and partly fill it with water from the can. A mix containing 1 bucket of cement, 2 of sand and 3 of stones will need about ¾ of a bucket of water, generally added in two or three stages during mixing.

Shovel the dry mix from around the outside of the heap into the crater until the water has been absorbed. Take care not to let the walls collapse, otherwise the water will flow away. Now turn the whole heap until it is evenly moist.

Form a fresh crater, as here, if more water is needed; alternatively, if only a little is required, sprinkle water sparingly on to the surface of the heap. As a general rule, use the smallest amount of water that will give a workable mix.

As a guide to workability, draw the shovel backwards over the heap in a series of jabs, trying to leave clear-cut ridges. These will be indistinct in a dry, crumbly mix; they will soon spread and level out in a mix that has had too much water added.

Using a concrete mixer

Small powered mixers are available from plant hire firms and do-it-yourself stores. They save time and effort and are easy to use; but, as the engines are sometimes temperamental, insist on seeing the machine started when it is delivered.

If the work is likely to extend over a considerable period, it is worth while considering the purchase of one of the small mixers now on the market as against hiring a powered one.

To use a powered mixer:
1. Start the engine.
2. Load the mixer with half the coarse aggregate and half the water.
(Measure all materials with a bucket.)
3. Add the sand and let it mix for a few moments.
4. Add the cement.
5. Add remaining coarse aggregate.
6. Check the consistency of the mix (if you need to handle it, stop the engine): add water to get a workable mix.
7. Continue mixing for a couple of minutes, then discharge the load into a wheelbarrow.

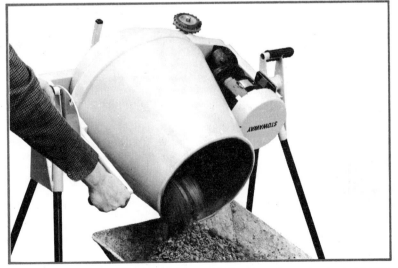

How to use a mixer. This electric concrete mixer can be collapsed to fit in the boot of a car, avoiding transport charges if the machine is hired. With all mixers, wash out the drum after each mix; scour with coarse aggregate and water at the end of the day. You may be charged heavily if the drum is returned dirty.

Concrete and cement/6

Preparation

If the soil where you plan to lay a path or drive is firm and compacted, lay the concrete directly on the ground.

Do not disturb the soil more than you have to. Dig out grass and weeds, level off bumps with a spade and roll the ground to provide a smooth, hard base.

If you want the surface of the concrete to be level with the surrounding ground, remove soil to the same depth as that of the proposed slab. On normal soils, make a concrete drive 100 mm. (4 in.) thick, a path 75 mm. (3 in.) thick.

If the soil is soft or loose, first put down a layer of rubble or stones and then compact it with a roller, removing extra soil to allow for this. Paths need only 25–50 mm. (1–2 in.) of rubble, drives 75 mm. (3 in.). Cover the rubble with sand and lay the concrete 100 mm. thick on a drive and 75 mm. on a path.

If there are only occasional soft spots in an otherwise firm base, make these up with well-compacted rubble.

If you propose laying fresh concrete on a cracked base, first break this up and compact the rubble with a roller. A new slab laid directly on the old base will almost certainly crack or scale

When the base is ready, set up the formwork—a frame to hold the concrete in place while it is hardening.

Cut the forms from sawn timber, 25 mm. thick and with a width equal to the intended depth of the slab.

Cheap timber or old floorboards are suitable for formwork, as the forms are removed once the concrete has hardened.

Support the forms with stout wooden pegs, 300–450 mm. (12–18 in.) long, driven into the ground.

When placing formwork for a drive or terrace on level ground, set the forms on one side slightly lower than on the other, to give the slab a slight slope for drainage.

Paths. Laying procedure is identical for both paths and, as shown below, drives.

Drives. Consider using ready-mixed concrete for a drive where access is easy.

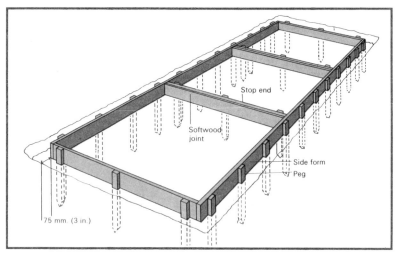

Setting out formwork. Prepare a base at least 75 mm. (3 in.) larger all round than the proposed size of the finished slab, so that the formwork can be placed on firm ground. Hammer the pegs in so that they are secure enough to resist sideways pressure of the concrete. Place joints on the side from which concreting will begin.

Laying step by step

1. Hammer in pegs on the outside of the formwork at about 1 m. (3 ft) intervals, with extra pegs where boards are butted together. Drive nails through the forms into the pegs. Leave no gaps between boards, otherwise concrete may flow out. The forms must be completely rigid to withstand pressure of compacted concrete.

2. Check the formwork with a spirit level. On a sloping site make sure that the side forms fall evenly by checking between them or the pegs. On a flat site make one side form 25 mm. (1 in.) lower than the other, so that the slab will slope for drainage. Put a 25 mm. wood strip on the lower side form, then check across for level.

3. Pour the concrete straight into the formwork, placing it as accurately as possible to minimise further handling. This is especially important if you are using ready-mixed concrete. Using rakes or shovels, spread the mix evenly to about 15 mm. above the formwork to allow for compaction with the tamping beam.

4. Tamp the concrete to compact it and give the slab a level surface. Use a heavy plank, fitting handles for a broad slab. Lift the plank a little and then drop it, moving it forward about half its thickness each time. Two passes should suffice. Then remove excess concrete by sliding the plank with a sawing action.

5. Insert expansion joints every 3 m. (10 ft) using 9 mm. softwood boards of the same length and width as the stop ends. Place each joint, with a knot-free edge uppermost, between the untamped concrete and the stop end. Joints can be placed before concreting begins, setting them on the side from which work will start.

6. Spread the concrete right up to the joint, compacting it thoroughly with the tamping beam and then removing the stop end and supporting pegs. Make sure that the joint remains vertical and that its top edge is level with the side forms and compacted concrete. Continue concreting on the far side of the joint.

7. Brush across the slab with a stiff broom if you prefer a rougher finish. In icy weather, a broomed surface is less slippery than the slightly rippled surface left by the final sawing motion of the tamping beam. For a smooth surface, finish with a wooden float, if necessary attaching this to a wooden handle.

8. Cover newly laid concrete with damp sacking, keeping it moist. Alternatively, use waterproof building paper or polythene sheets weighted down with bricks. Curing takes four days in warm weather, up to ten in winter. After this, the concrete can take light loads but keep heavy loads off for as long again.

Concrete and cement/8

Concreting alongside a wall

If laying a path alongside a wall or building you will be unable to use the tamping beam across its width. The solution is to lay the concrete in alternate bays, compacting and levelling it by using the tamping beam lengthways between stop ends.

When placing the formwork, insert a strip of bitumen-impregnated fibreboard, 12 mm. ($\frac{1}{2}$ in.) thick, to form a joint between the wall and the slab.

When laying the first bays, make sure that the stop ends are firmly fixed so that they cannot be displaced by the pressure of concrete.

Leave the stop ends in place while the concrete hardens; then remove them, stand on the hardened concrete, and fill in the empty bays. When all the concrete is hard, remove the side form.

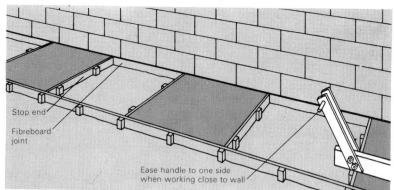

Stop end
Fibreboard joint
Ease handle to one side when working close to wall

Timber joints are unnecessary when laying alternate bays. Natural shrinkage when drying out leaves sufficient space for expansion and contraction. When levelling the second set of bays, stand on the hardened surfaces of the bays you laid first.

Working on sloped and curved sites

On a steep slope, lay as stiff a mix as possible to prevent the concrete from flowing during compaction; allow shorter spaces between stop ends.

For a curved path or drive, make the formwork out of 12–19 mm. ($\frac{1}{2}$–$\frac{3}{4}$ in.) thick boards, which are easy to bend. Set the supporting pegs close together.

If boards are 25 mm. (1 in.) thick, soak them for several hours before bending. Alternatively, make a series of saw cuts 6 mm. ($\frac{1}{4}$ in.) deep across the width of each board, bending the board so that the uncut face is in contact with the concrete.

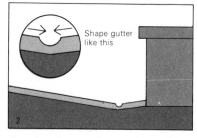

Rain-flow

Shape gutter like this

A slope away from a garage [1] presents no drainage problems. For a reverse slope [2], lay the slab to a point below floor level, then slope it upward to the door. Fashion the gutter by tamping with a piece of piping, making it slope away to one side.

How to cast your own slabs

The technique used for laying paths and drives can be adapted for casting your own slabs and blocks. Home-cast slabs and blocks are suitable for paths and dwarf walls in the garden, but they have no structural strength. Make them with a 1:3 mix of cement and sand.

Slabs must be at least 38 mm. ($1\frac{1}{2}$ in.) thick. Make the formwork 12 mm. ($\frac{1}{2}$ in.) deeper than the slab thickness required and spread 12 mm. of damp sand over the base before placing the concrete. This will make it easier to lift the slabs after they have hardened.

For a decorative finish use stone chippings instead of sand. A layer of exposed aggregate will be embedded in the cement, giving an attractive, non-slip surface.

Compact and level the concrete as for a path or drive and cover with damp sacking to prevent it drying out too rapidly.

Use a straight-edge as a guide when cutting

Cut with a trowel

Cut the slabs to size with a trowel one or two hours after pouring (the shorter time in warm weather). Slice right through the slab. To give blocks an informal finish, cut through only a third of the thickness, breaking at the trowel marks when lifting.

Leave the slabs or blocks to cure for four or five days, covering with damp sacks. Then lift carefully and stack them on edge.

Laying paving slabs

Remove 75–100 mm. (3–4 in.) of soil; level and roll the surface. If the soil is spongy, roll in a layer of hardcore and top with sand. Mark the path with string lines.

Bed each slab on five pats of stiff mortar —1 part cement to 3 parts sand. Set one pat under the middle of the slab and the others just inside the four corners.

Lay the slabs touching or with 12 mm. (½ in.) joints between. The former method saves work. For the second, insert a 12 mm. board to ensure even spacing.

Tap each slab lightly into the mortar bed (placing a block of wood under the hammer) until it has no tendency to rock and is level with adjacent slabs in each direction.

Fill open joints with wet mortar or dry cement–sand mix. If using wet mortar (as here) pack this into the joints, and trowel it to just below slab level.

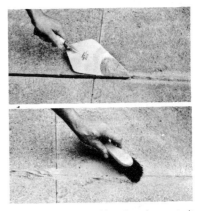

When filling joints with a dry mix, empty it in from the edge of the trowel, afterwards brushing away any surplus. Water the joints with a can and fine rose.

Making steps with paving slabs

Paving slabs make excellent treads for garden steps, with the risers formed from blocks or smaller slabs. If home-made slabs are used, they can be cast to exactly the required area and depth.

First decide how many steps are needed, basing your calculation on the distance between the upper and lower levels. Plan your steps so that each tread is at least 280 mm. (11 in.) deep (i.e. from front to back) and the risers not more than 175 mm. (7 in.) high. Suitable tread-riser combinations are shown in the diagram.

To support the riser of the first step, dig a trench 100 mm. (4 in.) deep and the same width as the proposed steps. Fill the trench with concrete to form a secure footing. When the concrete has hardened, lay small slabs to form the bottom riser, bedding these in 1 : 3 cement–sand mortar.

Firm and level the soil behind the riser, then lay a slab to form the bottom tread, on a similar mortar mix, so that the front protrudes 25 mm. (1 in.) beyond the riser.

Use the back of the tread as a base for the next riser. Lay the treads with a slight fall towards the front for drainage.

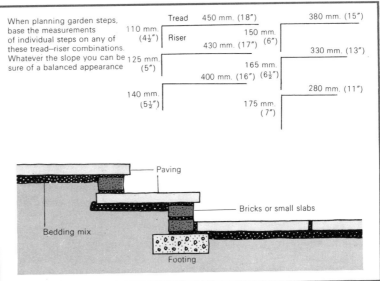

When planning garden steps, base the measurements of individual steps on any of these tread–riser combinations. Whatever the slope you can be sure of a balanced appearance

	Tread		
Riser 110 mm. (4½")	450 mm. (18")		380 mm. (15")
	430 mm. (17")	150 mm. (6")	
125 mm. (5")		165 mm. (6½")	330 mm. (13")
	400 mm. (16")		
140 mm. (5½")		175 mm. (7")	280 mm. (11")

Paving — Bedding mix — Bricks or small slabs — Footing

To build steps into a bank or a raised lawn, first cut out the rough outline of the steps, without loosening the remainder of the soil. Complete the cutting out as building proceeds. Build side walls to prevent the soil from spilling on to the steps.

Concrete and cement/10

Planning

Damp brick floors, or timber floors which have rotted, can be replaced with concrete. In a cottage with low ceilings, extra headroom can be gained by laying a concrete floor at a lower level than the existing floor. When converting a garage to give extra living space, new flooring may have to be laid to give a higher floor level.

Floor laying is more exacting work than laying a path. If you have no experience of concreting, get it done professionally. If you do it yourself, consult your council surveyor about building regulations.

If an existing solid floor is sufficiently lower than surrounding floors, lay the new slab over it. Otherwise, remove the floor and dig out the base. On soft ground, or when replacing a raised timber floor, place a layer of hardcore, topped with sand.

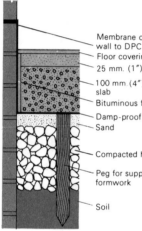

- Membrane carried along wall to DPC
- Floor covering
- 25 mm. (1") screed
- 100 mm. (4") concrete slab
- Bituminous felt joint
- Damp-proof membrane
- Sand
- Compacted hardcore
- Peg for supporting formwork
- Soil

Section through a concrete floor

Provide ducting for pipes and cables below the slab and remove plaster from the walls below the DPC (damp-proof course).

All concrete floors should have a damp-proof barrier. If a sound concrete floor is being used as a base for a new one, brush on two coats of a heavy damp-proofing liquid, e.g. Bituseal. In all other cases, lay 500-gauge polythene sheeting over the base before concreting, with the joints double-folded or bonded with adhesive.

For laying the slab you will need two 2 m. (6 ft) lengths of 125 × 75 mm. (5 × 3 in.) timber for the formwork, a 150 × 38 mm. (6 × 1½ in.) compacting board a little shorter than the width of the room, and a number of stout wooden pegs.

Use a mix made from 1 part cement, 2½ parts sand and 4 parts coarse aggregate.

Laying a screed

To give a completely level surface to the floor, lay a finishing screed on top of the slab, preferably placing it the same day or the next day. Use a 1:3 cement–sand mix, as stiff as possible.

You will need two strips of smooth, straight timber 25 mm. (1 in.) thick, a clean, smooth compacting board, a spirit level, a sheet of plywood on which to stand, and a steel float if the floor is to be left bare or a

Laying procedure

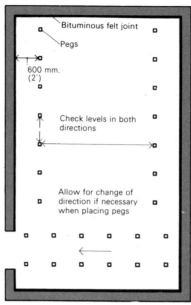

- Bituminous felt joint
- Pegs
- 600 mm. (2')
- Check levels in both directions
- Allow for change of direction if necessary when placing pegs

1. Drive in pegs, to support the formwork, while preparing the base and before laying the polythene. Place the pegs so that the forms can be drawn back to the exit.

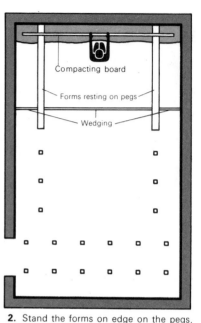

- Compacting board
- Forms resting on pegs
- Wedging

2. Stand the forms on edge on the pegs, wedging them across the room if necessary. Check levels, then lay a 1 m. (3 ft) strip of concrete as for an *in situ* path.

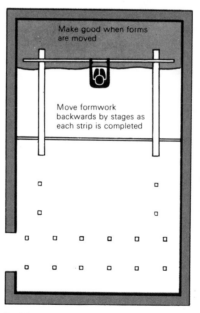

- Make good when forms are moved
- Move formwork backwards by stages as each strip is completed

3. Lift the forms, draw them back and rest on the next set of pegs. Fill and compact the spaces left by removal of the strips. Make good the surface with a float.

- Angle of work changed towards exit

4. Continue working backwards, checking levels often, so that you finish at the exit. Make sure at each stage that you can reach for compaction and making good.

wooden float if you plan to lay tiles or some other type of flooring.

If the slab is not freshly laid, wet it thoroughly. If newly laid, stand on the plywood. Place the 25 mm. timber strips in the same positions as the formwork used for laying the slab, spread the mix and level it with the compacting board.

Leave a scored surface if ceramic tiles are to be laid. A wooden float, with beer

bottle caps nailed to the face, will do this.

Draw the strips forward and make good, floating the surface with a trowel and checking levels frequently. Continue working backwards to the exit, changing the angle of work if necessary.

Leave the floor to cure for at least three days; if it is essential to cross the floor during this time, lay sheets of ply or blockboard.

What you can buy

Pre-cast concrete units range from garden ornaments and plant containers to building blocks and garage walls. All are made to standards that cannot be matched by do-it-yourself methods.

Pre-cast paving slabs save a great deal of work compared with concrete laid *in situ*. They are less liable to chip and crack than slabs cast at home.

Concrete lintels, designed to take the weight of blocks or bricks over windows and doorways, are available in stock sizes from 760 to 2750 mm. (2 ft 6 in. to 9 ft) in length. Other sizes can be ordered.

Among the more popular pre-cast units are the pierced, or openwork, blocks for building screen walls. Screen blocks, pilaster (pier) blocks and copings are made by a number of manufacturers, and the maker's instructions in the use of any particular block should be followed.

The most common size for screen blocks is $300 \times 300 \times 100$ mm. ($12 \times 12 \times 4$ in.). These are not bonded, as bricks are, but laid in line to give a recurring pattern.

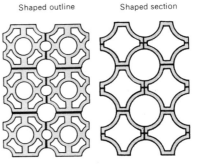
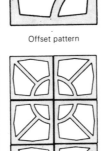

Centred pattern   Offset pattern   Shaped outline   Shaped section

Screen block patterns. Offset patterns form a composite design when correctly laid; others have scalloped edges, adding to the decorative effect. Screen walls can also be constructed from shaped sections which fit together to form a pattern.

Types of building blocks

There are two categories of building blocks —common and facing. Walls made of common blocks have to be rendered, those made of facing blocks do not.

Common blocks. Lightweight aggregate blocks are usually the best choice for general use. They will take nails and screws, can be chiselled for conduits and are suitable for walls of all types. They are made in both load-bearing and non-load-bearing grades.

Aerated blocks, e.g. Celcon or Thermalite, are also easy to work and have better insulation qualities but are more expensive and are unsuitable for exposed garden walls. Aerated blocks can be sawn and will take nails and screws.

Dense concrete blocks are heavier and have no special advantages for do-it-yourself work. However, they are suitable for use below the DPC of buildings (subject to local regulations).

Facing blocks. Split blocks have a surface resembling natural stone.

Profiled blocks are cast in patterned moulds. In exposed aggregate blocks, the colour and texture of the aggregate gives a decorative finish.

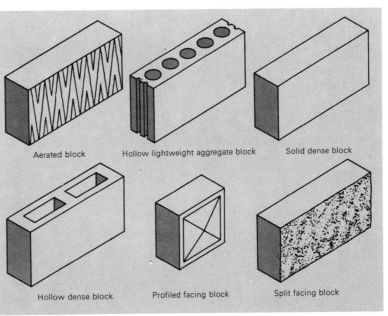

Aerated block   Hollow lightweight aggregate block   Solid dense block

Hollow dense block   Profiled facing block   Split facing block

Types of building blocks. The hollow blocks are lighter to handle and have a higher insulation value. Pipes and conduits can be run through the cavities.

Standard common-block sizes

Common blocks in general use are designed to course and bond with standard-sized bricks. The usual practice is to quote nominal sizes, which include 10 mm. ($\frac{3}{8}$ in.) for mortar joints on height and length and 5 mm. ($\frac{1}{4}$ in.) for rendering on the thickness on imperial blocks.

Thus, the actual dimensions of a nominal $450 \times 225 \times 225$ mm. ($18 \times 9 \times 9$ in.) block work out at $440 \times 215 \times 215$ mm. ($17\frac{5}{8} \times 8\frac{5}{8} \times 8\frac{5}{8}$ in.).

Make sure that your supplier realises that you are ordering nominal sizes.

Type of block	Height*	Length	Thickness
Dense	140 mm. ($5\frac{5}{8}$ in.) 215 mm. ($8\frac{5}{8}$ in.)	440 mm. ($17\frac{5}{8}$ in.)	50, 60, 75, 90, 100, 140, 190, 215 mm. (2, $2\frac{1}{2}$, 3, $3\frac{1}{2}$, 4, 6, $8\frac{3}{4}$ in.)
Lightweight aggregate	215 mm.	440 mm.	50, 60 mm. (non-load-bearing); 75, 90, 100, 140, 190, 215 mm. (load-bearing)
Aerated	140 mm. 215 mm.	440 mm. 515 mm. ($20\frac{1}{4}$ in.), 610 mm. (24 in.)	50, 60, 75, 90, 100, 140, 190, 215 mm.

*These heights will make level courses with the standard 65 mm. ($2\frac{5}{8}$ in.) brick. In northern England, dense blocks are also made 150 mm. ($6\frac{1}{4}$ in.) high, and all types 215 mm. ($9\frac{3}{8}$ in.) high, to course with the 73 mm. ($2\frac{7}{8}$ in.) deep bricks of that area.

Concrete and cement/12

Lightweight block walls

Concrete blocks are laid in much the same way as bricks, except that long block walls, instead of being bonded continuously, must have vertical movement joints every 6–9 m. (20–30 ft) of flexible mastic compound instead of mortar. These can be formed against door or window-frames.

Block walls also have to be reinforced with brick piers at intervals according to their dimensions (see table for maximum distances, and p. 9 for pier construction). The type of lightweight block to use depends on whether it is to be load-bearing and on the degree of insulation required.

Load-bearing strength varies between makes of blocks, but lightweight aggregate blocks generally offer maximum strength and aerated blocks the greatest insulation.

If maximum insulation is to be gained, it is important not to use blocks that are stronger than needed, because the strength depends largely on high density, whereas insulation is dependent on low density.

Check with your council's surveyor's office about building regulations before you build a block wall, and get advice from a surveyor or architect before you build a load-bearing wall.

To calculate the number of blocks needed, including half and three-quarter blocks for wall ends, openings and intersections, make a scale drawing showing the positions of individual blocks.

Metric blocks can be bought by the square metre, and imperial by the square yard, from builders' merchants. Allow extra for breakage.

Concrete blocks must be laid in a weak mortar, so that any cracking caused by shrinkage occurs in the mortar rather than in the blocks. Weak mortar is also needed between concrete blocks and other materials, such as brick or other types of concrete.

Manufacturers' recommendations for cement-lime mortars vary between 1:1:6 and 1:2:9 (see p. 4), so it is best to follow the advice given by the block maker.

Mortars of 1 part of masonry cement to 6 parts of sand, or 1 part of Portland cement to 6 parts of sand with plasticiser added, can also be used.

Set out and lay foundations as for bricklaying (see pp. 12–13). Lay the DPC between 10 mm. (⅜ in.) layers of mortar, as when bricklaying (see p. 15) but do not lay lightweight blocks below the DPC.

Check line and level constantly while laying the first course. Fill vertical joints and use a 10 mm. thick piece of wood to gauge the joint thickness.

Lay the second course with vertical joints centred between the joints below. Start from corners and intersecting walls, stretching the line between end blocks.

Prop door and window-frames in position (see p. 16) and build up to them. Screw galvanised frame cramps to the frame and set their tanged ends in the mortar joints.

Finish free-standing walls with dense-concrete coping slabs, to protect them against moisture penetration.

External faces of common block walls must be rendered (see p. 18) to keep out moisture. A 1:2:9 mix of cement, lime and sand is usually suitable, but in winter or on a severely exposed wall, a 1:1:6 mix may be needed.

Maximum dimensions for concrete block walls

Thickness of blockwork	Max. length between lateral supports, e.g. piers	Max. height for partition walls or infilling with top support	Max. height for free-standing walls
50 mm. (2″)	2400 mm. (8′)	2400 mm.	1200 mm. (4′)
60 mm. (2½″)	3000 mm. (10′)	3000 mm.	1500 mm. (5′)
75 mm. (3″)	3600 mm. (12′)	3600 mm.	1800 mm. (6′)
100 mm. (4″)	4500 mm. (15′)	4500 mm.	2200 mm. (7½′)
140 mm. (6″)	6000 mm. (20′)	6000 mm.	3000 mm. (10′)
215 mm. (8¾″)	7500 mm. (25′)	7500 mm.	3800 mm. (12½′)

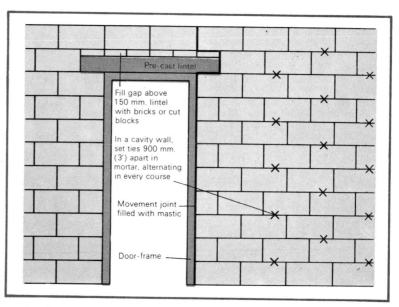

Pre-cast lintel

Fill gap above 150 mm. lintel with bricks or cut blocks

In a cavity wall, set ties 900 mm. (3′) apart in mortar, alternating in every course

Movement joint filled with mastic

Door-frame

Forming a doorway. The mastic-filled joint is unnecessary on short walls.

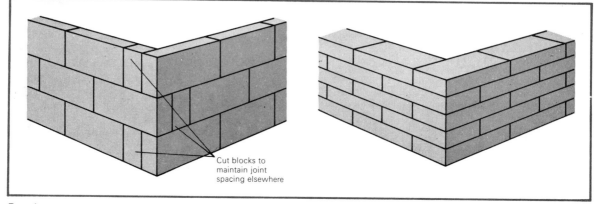

Cut blocks to maintain joint spacing elsewhere

Forming a corner with blocks. Build a thicker wall (right) by laying blocks on their faces.

Putting up a screen wall

Study carefully the block manufacturer's instructions about vertical strengthening and maximum distances between pilasters. For the foundations, dig a trench 300 mm. (1 ft) wide and 200 mm. (8 in.) deep. Cover base with 12 mm. ($\frac{1}{2}$ in.) of sand.

Fill the trench with Mix A (see p. 29), then compact the concrete thoroughly and eliminate air pockets by striking the surface, as here, with a stout post or batten. Check that the surface is level, using a spirit level on a straight-edge.

If strengthening is necessary, insert a length of reinforcement into the concrete before it sets. Insert another, not more than 3 m. (10 ft) from the first, remembering that an exact number of screen blocks nominal must fit between the pilasters.

Spread a bed of bricklaying mortar (1:5 masonry cement and soft sand) around each reinforcement or at the site of each pilaster. Position a pilaster block on each bed, line them up, then fill them with concrete Mix B (see p. 29).

Spread more mortar for jointing on each pilaster block, lay the next block on top and check for alignment. Fill the second laid block with Mix B, tamp it down and check for level. Add mortar for jointing, then position and fill a third block.

Spread mortar on the concrete base, to receive the first two screen blocks, and into the groove of one pilaster. Put one block in position against the pilaster mortar its upright edge, then mortar and position a second block.

Set a third screen block on top of the first one laid. Lay three blocks similarly against the other pilaster, then complete the first course working inwards from both ends. Check that each block is vertical before putting another in position.

Continue laying screen blocks until the required height is reached, making frequent checks that courses are level and straight. If the pilasters are not high enough, increase the height before laying any screen blocks above the third course.

Recess the jointing mortar with a strip of hardwood slightly thinner than the mortar joints and its end cut to an angle of about 45°. Run this along the vertical then the horizontal joints. Add coping and pilaster caps for finishing touches to wall.

Stone and stonework/1

Types of stone

Five kinds of natural stone are generally available for do-it-yourself work:

Granite: a hard, sparkling stone that polishes well and is non-porous. Expensive, it is generally available in grey, pink and brown. Typical kinds: Shap Pink, (grey-pink), Shap Blue (grey-blue).

Marble: a fairly hard stone that polishes well. Available in a range of colours with distinctive, free-flowing patterns. Suitable for fireplace surrounds, table tops and hearthstones. Typical kinds: Connemara (green), Bleu Belge (black and white).

Slate: dense, brittle and non-porous; easily split into thin laminations. Available in black, grey and green. Used outdoors mostly for damp-coursing, roofing and copings; indoors for decorative facings, hearthstones and sills. Fairly expensive. Typical kinds: Westmorland (green), Cornwall (grey), South Wales (black).

Limestone: a chalky stone that varies in hardness, durability and price. Colours range from buff, cream and ivory to brown and green. Used chiefly for paving, walls, steps and rockeries. Typical kinds: Portland (cream), Bath (dark cream), Purbeck (light grey).

Sandstone: strong and durable, the colour varying from red, pink and buff to green, brown and grey. Suitable for paving, sills and copings. Typical kinds: Forest of Dean (blue-grey), Lumshill (light brown).

Artificial stone: blocks and slabs closely resemble natural stone but are cheaper. Cast to exact sizes, they require no dressing. Some types are made by applying a facing of crushed stone and coloured cement to plain concrete blocks. Others use the same crushed stone aggregate throughout.

Artificial stone is known under various other names: 'cast', 'pre-cast', 'imitation' and 'reconstructed'. It can be obtained in a variety of colours, sizes and finishes and is used for both walling and exterior paving work.

Buying stone

Natural stone can be bought direct from a quarry, from a monumental mason, or from a horticultural merchant, in thicknesses from 25 mm. (1 in.) upwards, in any of three finishes:

Dressed: fully dressed stone is the most expensive, since it is supplied cut to your requirements. Each stone is squared up and has machined bed-faces.

Semi-dressed: the stones are cut to approximate sizes and the finishing work is left to the purchaser. This involves a certain amount of trimming and cropping with a sharp cold chisel and club hammer.

Undressed: the cheapest stone of all—simply chunks of the raw material from the quarry face. Use it as it is for rockeries and random walling: dressing it is difficult.

A square foot of York stone, 25 mm. thick, weighs about 6 kg. (13 lb.). A tonne covers about 7·5 sq. m. (9 sq. yds). For crazy paving, 1 tonne of broken slabs will cover about 9 sq. m. (11 sq. yds). Portland stone or Cotswold sawn offcuts are a little heavier and cover slightly less—roughly 7 sq. m. (8–9 sq. yds).

Dressed   Semi-dressed   Undressed

Stonemason's dictionary

Aggregate: the material used in conjunction with cement and sand, e.g. broken brick, stones, etc.

Bed-faces: the horizontal surfaces of stones that bear upon each other.

Bolster: a wide cutting chisel.

Bondstones: stones built into a free-standing wall for additional strength. *Throughs* go right across the wall; *headers*, or *bonders*, reach beyond the centre of the wall.

Dressings: a stone is 'dressed' when its surface has been cut or trimmed.

Hydrated lime: lime that has been mixed with water, dried out and then ground to a fine powder; used for making lime mortar.

Drilling, polishing and cleaning

Always use a carbide-tipped masonry bit for drilling stone with a power drill. Use the slower speed with a two-speed drill, or a speed reducer with a single-speed drill.

Drill in short sharp bursts, withdrawing at frequent intervals to prevent clogging and overheating of the drill bit.

Apply moderate pressure; too little may cause the cutting edge of the drill to chip.

For hand drilling, use a stardrill or a Rawldrill. Hammer the drill into the stone and twist it between blows to clear away chips.

Trim ragged edges of stone slabs with a sharp bolster and a club hammer, or use a sharp coarse rasp.

If you require polished stone for decorative purposes—for making a marble top or a slate hearth, for example—it is worth getting a mason, who has special equipment, to do the polishing. If you propose to tackle the job yourself, follow the appropriate procedure listed below:

Slate and marble: use an abrasive disc on a power drill. Pour water on to the surface to be polished, to act as a lubricant, then apply the abrasive disc in small, circular movements.

Soon dust particles will mix with the water to form a 'slurry' with the consistency of cream.

After a few minutes, clean off part of the slurry and the surface of the stone will be seen to be developing a sheen. When sufficiently polished, wash off the slurry and dry with a lint-free cloth. Finish with a colourless wax polish.

Slate can be given a coat of polyurethane varnish to seal the surface. Marble cannot, since the varnish yellows slightly in time and may spoil the marble's colours.

Granite can be polished in the same way by using carborundum and abrasive polishing powders, e.g. rouge, in the slurry.

Cleaning procedures differ for different types of stone.

Limestone and sandstone: the secret is to use a fibre scrubbing brush, plenty of fresh water and lots of energy. Avoid detergents, especially those which contain alkalis such as soda ash or caustic soda, since they break down the surface of the stone. The appearance of internal stonework can usually be improved by brushing the surface with a soft-haired brush to remove the dust.

Marble and granite: non-abrasive, acid-free detergents can be used to remove grease, provided all traces are rinsed off afterwards with fresh water. Wipe the surface clean, and polish with a chamois leather. Never use liquid detergent on marble flooring as this invariably leaves slippery patches on the surface. Clean the surface frequently with a soft brush to remove abrasive dust.

Slate: wash with hot water and a mild detergent. Rinse off and polish with putty powder, bought from a stonemason, on a soft felt pad.

Artificial stone: if the use of a moderate detergent fails to clean up the stone and the surface is reasonably flat, use a medium-fine pumice powder and a bristle scrubbing brush. Again, use plenty of fresh water.

Removing stains

Marble: most stains can be bleached out with a paste made from hydrogen peroxide (from the chemist) and powdered whiting (paint shop). Spread the paste over the stained area, add a few drops of ammonia, and keep the paste damp by covering it with plastic sheeting. Allow the paste to stand for a few minutes, then wash it off. Rinse with hot water, then polish.

Rust stains can sometimes be washed off with ammonia or a paste made from equal parts of amyl acetate and acetone mixed with whiting. Superficial scratches can be removed by using very fine wet-and-dry abrasive paper in its wet state.

Remove smoke stains by gentle scrubbing with powdered pumice and water. If the stains are persistent use either a cut lemon or carbon tetrachloride. Only use the latter in a well-aired place, since the fumes are dangerous.

Limestone and sandstone: a stone hearth that has been slightly burnt can be cleaned up by using a medium-grade glass-paper. Deep burns cannot be removed.

Remove the moss-coloured stains on garden ornaments by using a wet scrubbing brush and a little hydrated lime.

Surface finish and layouts

Select natural stone for paving work with care: many stones absorb water and when saturated or muddy can be dangerous to walk on. All artificial stone paving has a semi-rough, non-slip surface.

Paving can be laid in a variety of patterns, depending on the size and shape of the slabs. The simplest looking arrangement, where paving is laid in a straightforward grid-like pattern, is the most difficult, since the slightest irregularity in the jointing lines will spoil the appearance. Usually it is better to adopt one of the less formal patterns, a few of which are shown. Avoid mixing patterns within the same area unless they are defined by border stones or changes of level.

Broken slabs can often be bought direct from the quarry; otherwise, try your local authority or a builders' merchant.

Edge crazy paving with stones having one straight side, since small, irregular stones are more easily broken away. The principal thing to watch when laying crazy paving is to key in the random shapes without forming any continuous joint lines right across the path.

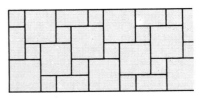

Grid pattern

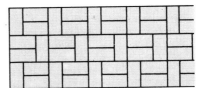

Stretcher pattern

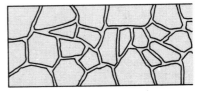

Random

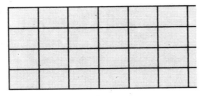

Dutch pattern

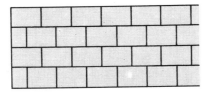

Court pattern

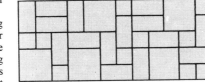

Crazy paving

Foundations

Remove topsoil to a slightly greater depth than the thickness of the slabs, and spread 15–25 mm. ($\frac{1}{2}$–1 in.) of bedding sand over the surface. Roll it in. If the soil is soft or loose, dig out an extra 75–100 mm. (3–4 in.) and spread a layer of hardcore, again finishing with sand and rolling.

For a paved drive, lay the slabs on a concrete base 75–100 mm. (3–4 in.) thick, placing the concrete on a hardcore foundation covered with bedding sand.

Levelling

Lay paths and patios with their surface sloping, to prevent rainwater from collecting in puddles. On level ground slope paths, garage drives and narrow strips of paving slightly to one side.

For patios a minimum slope of 40–50 mm. ($1\frac{1}{2}$–2 in.) in 3 m. (10 ft) is sufficient. Make sure the slope falls away from the house or other buildings in the vicinity.

If the area does not adjoin a building, slope it away in two directions.

Coloured jointing

A feature can be made of paving joints by colouring the mortar. Various proprietary additives are available and manufacturers' instructions should be followed carefully. Too great a proportion of colouring matter can upset the strength of the cement.

Often the appearance of paving is enhanced if white pointing is used. For this you need white Portland cement and some light or silver-coloured sand.

Laying

Dry laying: place the slabs on the bedding sand and tap them level with a mallet. Butt the slab edges close against each other or leave 15 mm. ($\frac{1}{2}$ in.) wide joints and fill with sand or a stiff 1:3 cement-sand mortar. When dry, this will brush off the surface and does not leave ugly staining.
Mortar-dab laying: use a 1:3 cement-sand mix for the mortar dabs, tapping each slab into position with a mallet and checking with a spirit level. Fill the joints as for dry laying, or butt together. Never run a roller over paving laid in this way.
Solid-bed laying: cover the hardcore base with a 20 mm. ($\frac{3}{4}$ in.) layer of blinding sand, and place this on a 25–50 mm. (1–2 in.) bed of 1:3 cement-sand mortar. Butt together or leave 5–10 mm. ($\frac{1}{4}$–$\frac{3}{8}$ in.) joints and fill with a stiff 1:3 cement-sand mortar finished flush with the surface.
Crazy paving: lay the stones on a 25 mm. (1 in.) bed of 1:3 cement-sand mortar, leaving joints 15–25 mm. ($\frac{1}{2}$–1 in.) wide. Select stones with straight edges for the borders, laying these first and filling in with smaller pieces. Check constantly with a spirit level and tap the stones in place. Fill the joints with a stiff mortar.

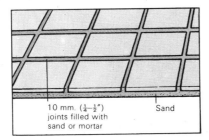

10 mm. ($\frac{1}{4}$–$\frac{1}{2}$") joints filled with sand or mortar — Sand

Dry laying: paving slabs are laid on sand. Suitable only for walking areas, since some settlement is likely to occur.

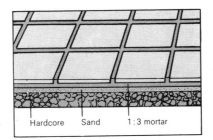

Hardcore — Sand — 1:3 mortar

Solid-bed laying: paving laid on a layer of mortar. Strong enough for drives.

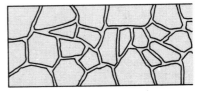

Mortar dabs —note spacing

Mortar-dab laying: paving laid on spots of mortar. Suitable only for walking areas, but will prevent settlement occurring.

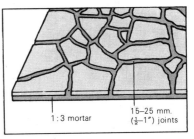

1:3 mortar — 15–25 mm. ($\frac{1}{2}$–1") joints

Crazy paving: slabs set on mortar bed. Drives need a 75 mm. (3 in.) concrete base.

Stone and stonework/3

Buying ready-to-build fireplace kits

Many manufacturers produce natural or artificial stone fireplaces which can be installed in place of an existing surround, whether the heating appliance is solid fuel, gas or electric.

It is worth visiting a Heating or Building Centre to compare designs. Prices range from £50 to £500, depending on the design, quality of stone and delivery distance involved.

Most manufacturers can either supply and install ready-made fireplaces from stock, or make them up to your own requirements, assisting you with the design and providing drawings free of charge.

Do-it-yourself fireplace kits are a cheaper solution. They contain everything you will require, from mortar and trowel to spirit level, and provide all stones cut to size and numbered to correspond with an assembly plan.

Most of the standard kits are 860 mm. (34 in.) high with an opening 530 mm. (21 in.) high × 425 mm. (16¾ in.) wide.

This sort of fireplace will take about a weekend to build, though if there is no existing appliance and surround to be removed beforehand, the job can easily be finished in a day.

'Method-built' fireplaces, manufactured by E. H. Bradley & Sons Ltd., Okus Quarries, Swindon are a third possibility. Instead of individual stones, the kit consists of several cast sections which have only to be cemented together. This type can be erected in an hour by two people.

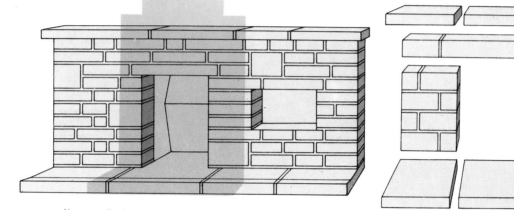

New stone fireplaces need not have the same proportions as the old

Jointing is kept to a minimum with fireplace kits

Building to your own design

Designing your own fireplace—including selecting and buying the stone—and then building it, can be a satisfying job.

Showrooms and magazines demonstrate the range of designs that are possible, and the bonding they require. When you have chosen a style appropriate to your room, prepare a design drawing for your own construction.

Draw it to scale on a sheet of graph paper—preferably with large squares subdivided into 100 smaller squares, and let each small square represent 10 mm. Or use paper with 12 squares to the inch so that 1 in. can represent 1 ft.

1. Draw in to scale the size of the existing fireplace opening.
2. Draw in the outline of the proposed surround.
3. Lightly sketch in the large stone (lintel) which bridges the fireplace opening.
4. Sketch in the remainder of the stones, taking care to avoid continuous vertical joint-lines running through from one course to another. The stones are best kept to an average of 50–200 mm. (2–8 in.) high, and 125–225 mm. (5–9 in.) wide. The depth of all the stones should be the same—about 125 mm. (5 in.). Mark in the hearthstone and the stone mantelshelf.
5. Give each stone a separate number. Corresponding numbers will be drawn on the stones by the mason to identify their positions when you come to build.
6. Finally put in the overall dimensions, which will help the mason to give you a price estimate.

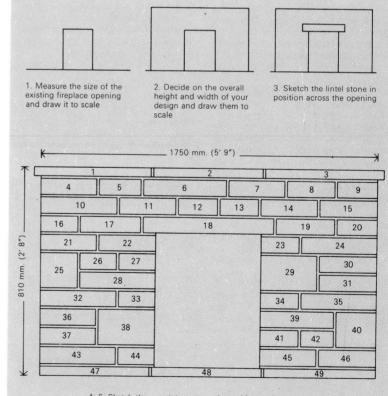

1. Measure the size of the existing fireplace opening and draw it to scale

2. Decide on the overall height and width of your design and draw them to scale

3. Sketch the lintel stone in position across the opening

4–6. Sketch the remaining stones in position and number them

Repointing

Crumbling mortar joints in old brickwork allow moisture to penetrate the wall. The remedy is repointing—clearing out the old mortar joint to a depth of about 12 mm. (½ in.) and replacing it with a new one. Should it be necessary to repoint the whole wall, the job can be done in stages, tackling about 1 sq. m. (1 sq. yd) at a time and completing the whole wall when you can. Always set up a platform for high walls, so that you work at chest level—do not try working on a ladder.

When repointing, you should match the composition of the new mortar to the old. If you do not know the mix for the old mortar, make the new mortar of 1 part lime to 1 part cement and 6 parts builders' sand (1:1:6).

Pointing trowel. Looks like a smaller version of the bricklayer's trowel; used for putting mortar into the joints.

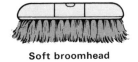

Hawk. Used to hold the mortar as you work; home-made from a piece of 225 × 225 × 12 mm. wood, with a handle underneath.

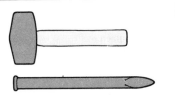

Plugging (jointing) chisel. A cold chisel ground to a pointed end; used for clearing out the old mortar; also needed—a club hammer to hit it with.

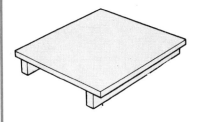

Spot-board. For holding a reserve of mortar.

Soft broomhead

Frenchman. For cutting off excess mortar when making a weather-struck joint. Make one from an old kitchen knife—file the end to a point, heat the tip, then bend the first 10 mm. (⅜ in.) at a right angle to the rest of the blade.

Straight-edge. Home-made from a piece of batten with a square of hardboard fixed to each end, so that when held against a wall it stands slightly away. Used in weather-struck joints for cutting off mortar in straight lines, allowing the droppings to fall down between straight-edge and wall.

Types of joint

If you are patching a wall, match the new joints with the existing ones. For example, form flush joints on a wall which already has them.

If you are completely repointing, or putting joints in new brickwork, use any of the joints shown here.

Weather-struck joints give the maximum protection from damp and so are worth the extra trouble, especially on chimneys and house walls.

Recessed joints look effective with rough textured bricks; flush or rubbed joints are better with smooth-surfaced ones.

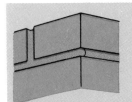

Rubbed joint—formed by rubbing with a semicircular piece of metal (see bricklaying sequence, p. 15)

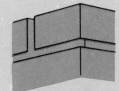

Recessed joint—scraped out with a pointed piece of metal and smoothed with a stick.

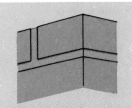

Flush joint—formed by rubbing with an old piece of sacking.

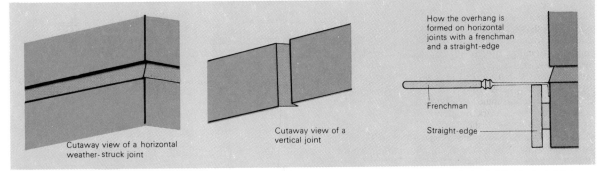

Cutaway view of a horizontal weather-struck joint

Cutaway view of a vertical joint

How the overhang is formed on horizontal joints with a frenchman and a straight-edge

Frenchman

Straight-edge

Weather-struck joint. This gives a sloped surface to allow rain to run off quickly. The horizontal joint is recessed under the top brick and slightly overhangs the lower one. The mortar is pushed into the horizontal joints with a pointing trowel. Excess mortar is cleaned off with a frenchman and a straight-edge lining up with the top of the brick. Vertical joints are sloped from one side to the other, matching the horizontal ones. These vertical slopes are formed with the trowel.

Repointing

Suitable case for treatment: a brick wall with badly deteriorated joints allowing rain to penetrate it. Before starting work, lay a sheet of polythene to protect the paving underneath from mortar droppings.

Use a plugging chisel and a club hammer to clear out the old mortar from about 1 sq. m. (1 sq. yd) of wall Clear vertical joints, then horizontal ones, to a depth of 10–15 mm. ($\frac{1}{2}$ in.).

Brush the joints down to remove dust and old mortar, then flick water over the wall with the brush. Soak the brickwork, so that it will not absorb the moisture from the new mortar when it is laid.

Mix up enough mortar on the spot-board for about two hours' work, and then load the hawk from it. Practise picking up mortar from the hawk, with a smooth upward sweep of the back of the trowel.

Force mortar into the joints—the uprights first, then the horizontals above and below. For weather-struck joints, form the slope as you go; for other joints, leave the mortar flush with the bricks.

Complete weather-struck joints by first neatening the uprights with a trowel. The mortar will already have a rough slope on it and any excess is now trimmed off neatly with a pointing trowel.

Next, use the frenchman to cut off the excess mortar at the bottom of the horizontal joints only. Use a straight-edge as a guide and run the frenchman along with the angled tip pointing downward.

When the mortar has become quite hard, brush off the rest of the waste from the area you have been working on. Then go on to the next square yard, clean out and repoint it, and so on.

To form a flush joint, wait until the mortar is semi-stiff and then rub a piece of sacking in one direction along the joint until it is flush with the brickwork. Brush off the waste when dry.

To form a recessed joint, use a piece of metal with a pointed, curved end, and a piece of wood the width of the joint.

Use the piece of metal to scrape the mortar from both vertical and horizontal joints to a depth of about 6 mm. ($\frac{1}{4}$ in.).

Rub the joint down gently with the piece of wood, so that the surface of the mortar is smooth and water-resistant.

Damaged brickwork

Brick, being porous, takes in moisture during rain, then allows it to evaporate in dry weather.

In winter, moisture may freeze inside the bricks; and when water turns to ice, it expands. This can cause the poorly made brick to 'spall'—that is, crumble at the edges. Once this process starts, the brick offers less resistance to the weather, and the crumbling speeds up.

Chip out decayed brick with a bolster and club hammer. Protect your eyes against flying chips with safety glasses or driving goggles. Cut back to solid brick, then use a narrow cold chisel to go even deeper into the mortar joints. Remove loose material with a wire brush.

If you cut back a brick to half its original width, leaving a hole 40 mm. (1½ in.) deep, you can replace the face of the brick with a queen closer.

This is a brick cut in half along its length, and once it is in position, there is no way of telling that it is not a whole brick. Cutting a queen closer is a highly skilled job, so take a matching brick and ask a builder to cut it for you if you cannot do it yourself.

In some cases you may have to remove whole bricks. This is not too difficult if you attack the pointing around the brick until you are in to brick-depth.

By this time the brick will usually vibrate free, and you can wiggle it out and clean the hole to take a new matching brick.

After patching, a wall may not look attractive—in which case render it or paint with stone or cement paint.

At the very least, it is worth while treating the wall with a good water repellent, applied liberally. This will ensure that frost does not get a chance to damage the brickwork again.

Where brickwork is damaged at ground level, or perhaps below, rake away the soil and remove all damaged bricks with a bolster and club hammer.

Make an 'apron' of rendering over the area and all along the base of the wall, about 450 mm. (18 in.) high, to give protection against rain splashes. Add a water-proofing liquid, or a powder such as Pudlo, to your mortar; or use the normal mix and treat the rendering with a water repellent.

Decayed stonework

Most natural stones do not flake as much as brickwork; but the softer sandstones and limestones are more vulnerable. Some stones can decay through chemical attack by impurities in the atmosphere, and stone preservatives are available for treating areas where such decay has only just started.

Where decay is serious, cut out the damaged stone with a bolster and club hammer and remove all loose debris.

To insert a new stone, use a mortar of 1 part cement to 4 of soft sand and add a PVA bonding liquid to the water in your mix.

Dampen the stone before you insert it, so that the mortar will not dry out too quickly.

If you cannot get matching stone, you will have to rely on mortar with dry pigment added to match the colour of the stone as nearly as possible.

Crushed stone is an ideal material to mix with cement, and a good mix is 12 parts of crushed stone to 3 of cement. Try a small area first, to see how the mortar looks when dry: you may have to make adjustments in the colouring.

If you have had to make deep cuts and no stone is available, bed slips of clay tile in the mortar to build up the hole ready for a final rendering.

Larger areas can be built up with expanded metal laths, and you can prepare any shaping of cornices and mouldings with 5 mm. (3/16 in.) mild steel rods bent to shape and secured by masonry pins driven into sound masonry.

Use galvanised wire to tie everything together at cornices, and treat the steel rods with a cold galvanising paint to prevent rusting when the mortar is applied.

Build up mortar on the frame, coat by coat, until the repair is complete.

You can make highly effective repairs on small damaged areas with one of the new epoxy-based fillers designed for concrete work.

These give an extremely strong bond, making them ideal for repairs to steps, especially worn treads, but they are expensive.

To protect stone from impurities in the air, it is a good idea to scrub it with cold water from time to time. Do not add acids, chemicals or detergents to the water.

If walls are very grimy, you would be well advised to call in a firm which specialises in stone cleaning. They normally use steam under pressure.

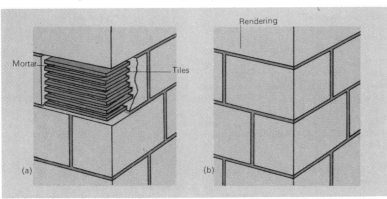

Deep stonework repair: (a) decayed stone cut away and tiles bedded in mortar; (b) hole filled and rendered flush with surrounding stonework.

Restoring a cornice, using expanded metal lath as a key for the mortar.

Efflorescence

This is the name given to a whitish fluff which sometimes appears on the surface of brickwork and the surrounding joints.

It is caused by water-soluble salts in the brick being drawn to the surface, where they crystallise.

New buildings, where a lot of water has to evaporate from brickwork and plaster, are most prone to this condition, but it may also occur in older property during heavy rain or after flooding.

The trouble is in no way serious on outside brickwork; it just looks messy.

It can be a nuisance indoors, as deposits may push wallpaper off the wall.

The normal treatment outdoors is to brush deposits with a wire brush until they no longer appear. Do not wash them away, as this will only aggravate the problem.

For inside redecoration, ask your builders' merchant for one of the proprietary liquids that penetrate the brick and neutralise the salts.

Persistent trouble may indicate serious dampness, perhaps even faults in a damp-proof course. In this case, the damp will have to be dealt with.

Settlement

Settlement is caused by movement of the ground beneath the house. There may be underground subsidence due to mining, or the ground may have been made up—possibly as a rubbish tip—and not given enough time to settle. Settlement can cause trouble in a house on the side of a hill, if there is land movement down the slope.

Trouble can be caused by building on clay subsoil, which moves according to the amount of water in the ground: during a prolonged drought, the clay dries out and shrinks. Soil around the foundations may be eroded by flooding.

Tree roots can be a special problem. The root system of the average tree has a coverage roughly equal to the spread of its branches. Roots close to wall foundations draw moisture from the ground and can cause the foundations to shrink and move.

Rotting and dying timber also loses volume, which in turn may cause movement in the soil. It is unwise to have large or fast-growing trees near your walls. If you are in doubt about trees, your local borough surveyor will advise you.

Warning signs

Running cracks on outside walls usually indicate settlement trouble. They are most apparent where an extension has been built on, or where a garage or a garden wall meets the house wall.

There may also be cracks around door tops and window-frames.

The first thing is to establish whether the movement has stopped. This may well be so with a new house which, once bedded down, will give no further trouble—though if, for example, a corner of the foundations has been undermined, movement may continue.

To find out, you can use one of two simple tests on outside walls.

Choose a crack, and at a fairly wide point bridge it with a piece of glass fixed with epoxy resin adhesive such as Araldite. Glass has little tensile strength, and the slightest new movement will crack it.

The second test is to bridge the crack with plaster of Paris. It will soon harden, and will crack if there is any movement.

These tests may have to extend over some months before you see results. Results can often be seen quicker if the cracks are repeated on inside walls. If the trouble is caused by building on clay, you may see cracks in the wallpaper open and close with the weather.

Dealing with settlement cracks

There is very little you can do about serious settlement cracks without having expensive underpinning carried out. Patching with filler will not help.

If you find, by testing, that there is serious movement, call in experts in foundation work. This is no job for an amateur.

Some firms use modern jacking methods to support structures while they put in new foundations, and this can reduce costs considerably, but it is an expensive busi-

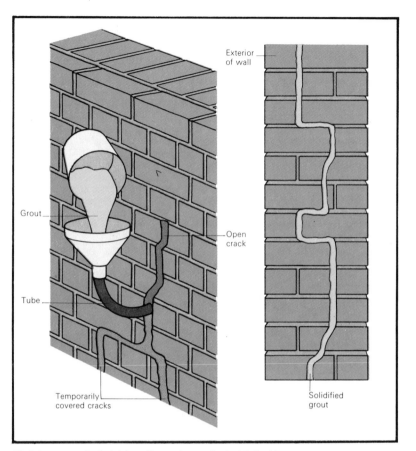

Shrinkage cracks in brick walls can be repaired with liquid grout.

ness to stop a house from moving. Cracks in masonry are not necessarily due to movement in the foundations. In a new property, there may be a fair amount of shrinkage due to drying out.

Shrinkage

Shrinkage cracking seldom occurs in clay bricks. It occurs most often in concrete and sand-lime bricks, and the critical time is during the first really long dry spell after a house has been built.

Shrinkage often appears as step-like cracks following the horizontal and vertical joints, and sometimes as a vertical crack through both brick and joint.

The cracks seldom extend below the damp-proof course, and there is no distortion of the brickwork.

Dealing with shrinkage cracks

These cracks, though unsightly, are not serious. Once movement has stopped, they can be repaired by raking out the joints, removing any cracked bricks, and re-pointing the brickwork.

For this, use a mortar made of 1 part cement, 2 of lime and 9 of well-graded soft sand. Carry out repairs during a spell of dry weather when the brickwork is dry.

In cases where it is difficult to point cracks with a trowel, feed a grout mix into the fissure.

Temporarily cover the wider parts of the

crack with soft clay, Plasticine, or even with a fabric-based adhesive tape. Then pour grout into the top of the crack, using a funnel and piece of plastic tube. The grout must be liquid enough to pour freely, yet not so wet that it trickles out at the base.

Get the tube as far into the wall as possible, even if it means enlarging the hole at the top a little with a cold chisel and club hammer.

After a few hours, when the grout has partly set, remove the temporary covering and neatly point the surface of the crack.

To cover up cracks in the bricks themselves use mortar dyed with pigments, such as those in the Feb range: by careful mixing it is possible to make the pointing almost invisible.

You can make a mortar using powdered brick of similar type to those in the wall, but this is difficult.

Having done your repair work, allow a waiting period to see that all is well. If the cracks open up again, it is time to call in expert advice.

Shrinkage cracks around window- and door-frames may be caused by the shrinkage of timber and not by movement of the brickwork.

In this case, the remedy is to point the cracks with a mastic sealing compound which will move with any slight movement between the materials.

Repairing chimney stacks

Chimney stacks, being well out of reach, are often neglected. Such neglect is dangerous, for high winds can dislodge a damaged stack.

You can make a fair check on a stack by standing well back and examining it through binoculars.

Look for leaning brickwork, serious cracks, missing or damaged pots, missing pointing and damaged flaunching.

To reach a stack, you need an extension ladder secured to the fascia board by a large screw-eye and rope. Then you must have a roof ladder of the type which hooks over the roof ridge.

If you are inexperienced, it can be highly dangerous working with ordinary ladders lashed together.

Brickwork cracked and leaning. If, on close examination, you find that the stack is in a dangerous state, call in professional help. It is not within the scope of the average handyman to remove and rebuild a stack without elaborate scaffolding.

Brickwork with crumbling and missing pointing. Rake out all loose and crumbling mortar from one face of the stack at a time, to a depth of 12–20 mm. ($\frac{1}{2}$–$\frac{3}{4}$ in.).

Dampen the joints, and repoint with mortar. The simplest to use is dry-mix mortar, available from most builders' merchants. All you need to add is water.

Bring the mortar slightly above the level of the brickwork, and form weather-struck joints (see Repointing, pp. 43–44).

If you want to mix your own mortar, use a mix of 3 parts of soft sand to 1 of cement. A little PVA adhesive added will make the mix easier to work. You can get this by the can from builders' merchants.

Loose bricks. Provided the main part of the stack is sound, remove mortar from around the brick with a cold chisel and club hammer. Ease the brick out and go down to the ground again to clean it up. Scrape all loose and crumbling mortar from the hole.

Wet the brickwork, add new mortar, and press the brick back in place. When it is set, repoint the brickwork.

Damaged flaunching. If the flaunching-mortar around the chimney pots is cracked

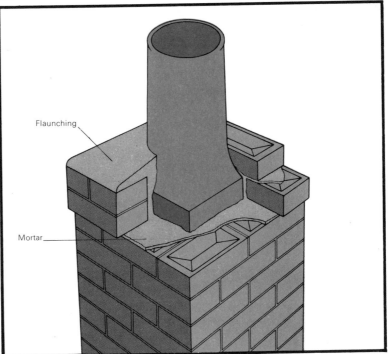

Flaunching should fit tightly around a chimney pot to throw off the rainwater.

and pulling away, carefully remove it with a club hammer and a cold chisel.

Collect the pieces by hand and put them in a bucket hooked on to your ladder—do not let them bounce off down the roof.

Try not to disturb the pots, but if you do break into the flue, it is advisable to seal off the fireplaces below, in case soot and mortar pieces fall down.

Clean away all loose material, then damp the work and repoint, sloping the mortar from the centre down, so that the surface sheds rain.

If you do not use a ready-mix, a mix of 3 parts of soft sand to 1 of cement plus a little PVA will do.

Broken chimney pot. Be careful: chimney pots are heavier than they look, so do not let one catch you off balance.

Block off the fireplaces indoors in case

soot falls; then carefully chisel away the flaunching from around the pot.

As soon as the pot starts to loosen, secure it with a stout rope looped around the stack. It is a good idea to get a helper on the roof to hold one end of the rope.

Ease the pot from its foundation and lift it off, using the rope to lower it to the ground.

Clean loose material away from the hole and bring up the new pot. Pack it with pieces of slate until it stands upright.

Then fill in around the pot with mortar, making sure that it gets into the gaps between the base of the pot and the brickwork. Do not let mortar go down the flue. Trowel the new mortar to a slope.

Incidentally, this is the time to fit a cowl if you have trouble with down-draughts or poor up-draughts.

Dealing with condensation

With the introduction of modern boilers, loss of heat up the flue has been very considerably reduced. This means that flues stay relatively cool, and gases and moisture are deposited on the flue walls in the form of condensation.

These deposits are highly corrosive and they soon destroy the flue lining, percolating through to the brickwork and eventually staining the chimney, destroying the pointing and weakening the whole stack.

On the outside of the stack you may see brownish patches. The deposits may also appear on internal walls as a sticky, brown liquid with an unpleasant smell. The only cure for this trouble is a new flue-lining.

Lining the flue. This is a job best left to the

professional unless you have had considerable experience.

Lining kits, which are usually in the form of a long flexible tube, can be obtained from most builders' merchants. If the merchant cannot also supply details about installation of the kit, they can be obtained from the supplier.

Stained chimney breast. If an inside wall is spoilt by deposits seeping through from a chimney, seal the surface with two coats of good quality aluminium sealer. This will prevent the deposits from bleeding through.

Alternatively, coat the wall in aluminium foil, sticking it in place with a rubber-bitumen coating. Then apply a

lining paper before repapering or painting.

Reducing condensation. With the flue lined, you can reduce the amount of condensation by seeing that your fuel (if you use solid fuel) is stored in a dry place; that you don't load the fire with vegetable peelings and other damp refuse; and that the top of the chimney is capped to prevent excessive rain from getting down it.

You can cap the pot with a half-round tile cemented in place or with a special pot-capper.

Unused chimneys. If you block up a fireplace, be sure to set a ventilator in the panel blocking it off, and to cap the chimney pot at the top. This will prevent condensation in the unused flue.

Problems with concrete

Paths and drives

To repair a chipped or flaking surface, chisel out the area to a depth of 20–25 mm. (¾–1 in.), undercutting the edges. Apply a PVA (polyvinyl acetate) compound, such as Clam No. 7, to the section and fill with a 1:3 cement–sand mortar with PVA added to it. Keep the mix as dry as possible.

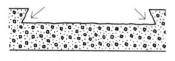

Undercut the damaged edges when chiselling out a damaged patch. Feathered edges (below) give less grip

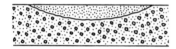

The amount of PVA, which gives a stronger bond, is specified on the container.

Patching almost invariably shows, and similar flaking will probably appear elsewhere. A new slab may be the only long-term solution.

When repairing the edge of a concrete slab, peg temporary formwork in place to support the fresh concrete while it hardens.

As fresh concrete is easily damaged, protect all edges and corners until the concrete is thoroughly cured. If damage does occur, the edges of the damaged section will usually be feathered, i.e. shallow and tapered. Deepen the edges with a chisel, undercutting if possible, and roughen the surface to provide a key.

Make good with a 1:3 cement–sand mortar, as dry as possible, tamping it firmly and finishing with a trowel. Protect the repair until it has cured.

Straight cracks which occur along construction joints are caused by normal expansion and contraction. Crooked cracks occurring elsewhere are due to poor construction. Unless severe, it is best to ignore them; if, however, the slab settles unevenly, so that a step appears at the crack, usually the only remedy is to break up the paving and replace it with a properly laid slab.

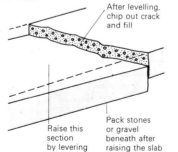

After levelling, chip out crack and fill

Raise this section by levering

Pack stones or gravel beneath after raising the slab

However, if the sunken section consists of less than 1 m. (1 yd) of narrow path, it may be possible to lever it up by inserting crowbars on either side and packing stones or gravel beneath to raise the slab to its correct level.

Uneven flagstones

Use a crowbar or strong spade to lever up one end of the slab. To avoid lifting a heavy slab, slip a broomstick or a length of piping under the raised end and roll the slab clear.

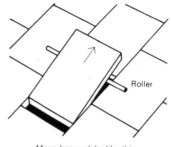

Roller

Move heavy slabs like this

If the slab was laid on sand, level the surface and make good with extra sand. If laid on mortar pats, replace the old pats with fresh mortar.

Damaged steps

Where a single lump of concrete has broken off the corner of a step, either cement the old lump back into place or fill in the corner with fresh concrete. Use a PVA adhesive whichever way you do the repair.

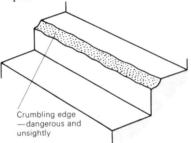

Crumbling edge —dangerous and unsightly

To repair a crumbling edge, chip away a V-shaped section and place a wooden support against the riser. Apply a PVA adhesive to the cut-out and add some to a 1:3 cement–sand mortar for filling. Cover the repair with damp sacking until dry.

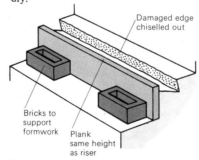

Damaged edge chiselled out

Bricks to support formwork

Plank same height as riser

Damaged rendering

If cement-based rendering flakes off a wall, the rendering itself is probably defective and the trouble will recur elsewhere.

As the weakness may extend a good way from the visible damage, chip the rendering well back from the crack or patch and leave the edges square. Wire-brush the undersurface and either score with a chisel or chase out mortar joints to provide a firm key.

Apply a dryish mortar of 1:1:6 cement–lime–sand, or the equivalent masonry cement–sand mix, using a PVA compound to improve bonding.

Repairs can be disguised by painting the whole wall.

Cracks in walls

Seek professional advice if severe cracks occur in concrete walls.

Repair minor cracks in the joints by chiselling out the mortar to a depth of 15 mm. (½ in.) and repointing.

There is nothing you can do to repair cracks in the blocks themselves, apart from filling with a non-shrinking cellulose plaster, such as Polyfilla, where the cracks carry through into the rendering or plastering. Such damage shows that too much cement was used in the mortar, which made the joints stronger than the blocks.

Cracks in floors

Minor cracks in concrete floors can be hidden with vinyl or other floor covering. If the surface is rough or slightly uneven, apply a self-smoothing screed, such as Smoothtex, before laying the covering.

If a floor has settled unevenly on either side of the crack and has produced a step, the only solution is to replace the floor. New cracks will occur in the same places if the existing floor is covered with fresh concrete.

'Dusty' concrete floors

There are several proprietary brush-on sealing compounds, e.g. Sealocrete, that will improve old or poorly finished floors which continually produce fine dust, provided that this is not excessive.

The alternatives are to cover the surface with vinyl or similar flooring, or to lay an entirely new floor.

Protection

Protect setting cement against damage by heavy rain with a framework of battens and a covering of heavy polythene sheeting. Protect against frost by covering the concrete or mortar as soon as it is set with a sheet of polythene, then a layer of straw, sand or earth, and another polythene sheet weighted down securely at the edges.

Repairs to walls and rendering can be protected by suspended polythene weighted down at the bottom edges.

Rapid-hardening cement

For work requiring high strength quickly, such as a repair to the bottom of a drain-pipe gulley, use aluminous cement, generally known as ciment fondu. This reaches full strength in very little time, so the mixing instructions must be carefully followed. Never mix ciment fondu with Portland cement or use it in contact with Portland cement concrete or mortar.